PICTURES
IN THE
DOLPHIN
MIND

PICTURES
IN THE
DOLPHIN
MIND

Frank Robson

SHERIDAN HOUSE

By the same author:

Thinking Dolphins, Talking Whales (1976)
Stranded (1984)

First published
in the United States of America 1988 by

Sheridan House Inc.,
145 Palisade Street
Dobbs Ferry, NY 10522

ISBN   0 911378 78 2

Printed in Singapore

Dedication

As much as the dedication of this book could be shared by many, I feel that, had it not been for the love and tolerance shown me by my wife throughout our life together, I would never have endured the mental stress and physical demands required to assist animals to help themselves in their fight for survival. In addition to this, she has presented me with a family equally tolerant, helpful and concerned for animals. And so, to Sal, my dear wife of fifty-six happy years, I dedicate this book.

Acknowledgements

The acknowledgements associated with this book could fill another entire paperback.

To the beach spotters and those involved in whale and dolphin rescue go my gracious thanks. Without your vigilance, concern and assistance I could have achieved but little in this field of endeavour.

To Capt. Morzer Bruyns, Dr Peter van Bree and Dr Dudoc van Heel of the Netherlands I give my thanks for their support and encouragement to collect and research cetacean specimens grounded on New Zealand coasts in the past twenty-five years.

Thanks also to Bill Rossiter, vice-president of Connecticut Cetacea International; Christine Stevens, president of the Animal Welfare Institute, Washington, D.C.; and the Australian Museum for their generous funding when the chips were down. Also to Project Jonah New Zealand for their support in getting the Marine Mammals Protection Act into the statute books, in addition to financial contributions to allow me to continue. To Nan Rice of South Africa for her support and contributions; and to those who have contributed photos as proof of events. And to all those people involved who I've failed to mention go my sincere and heartfelt thanks.

To Kay Mooney for her voluntary help with the original manuscript some four years ago, which has now for obvious reasons been rewritten and brought up to date by the voluntary efforts of Rosamond Rowe, a longtime student in whale rescue; to these two caring souls go my heartfelt thanks for recording in words my experiences of a lifetime which, without their input, could have escaped publication. Many, many thanks, Kay and Ros.

Sincere thanks also to Jan Kite and Judith Gannaway, who stepped in at short notice to assist with typing the final draft.

And last, but by no means least, I wish to thank publicly our son Bruce for his instant response to help me on the beaches at any hour of the day or night during the past twenty-five years. Many grounded whales have him to thank for the help rendered them.

Contents

Looking to nature for
the answers

I've always had an affinity with animals, starting from the time when the family dog was my nurse.

Nip and I came into the family at about the same time. I was the second child and he was the payment for my father's treatment of a sick animal. My father was the first Hawke's Bay Acclimatisation Society ranger — and, at the time, the only one. He was in charge of the society's fish ponds, bird pens and animal enclosures as well as being required to go out on his bike after poachers and other transgressors.

My mother was his assistant and deputy so Nip the cocker spaniel became my guardian. He was left in charge of me while my mother helped with feeding and caring for the stock. If I cried Nip barked and Mother came running. It was a good system and the beginning of my life of close rapport with animals.

As an only son with four sisters I found that the house tended to be a woman's world and so the animals became my real friends. I realise now that even then I must have been communicating mentally with them, even though I thought I was using the spoken word only. I just knew that I was happy in their company and they in mine and that I understood their needs.

It was a great stroke of luck to be born into a naturalist's family. My father had an inherent skill and knowledge about living things and, although he never gave it a thought, I believe he had the gift of mental communication. He was expert at keeping animals alive and happy, and if one of them died his search for knowledge led him to carry out an autopsy with an untaught surgeon's skill.

1

Life with my father and the stock in his charge was an adventure of discovery. He was running his own six hectare farm at Taradale and it took this plus his job as ranger and curator of the Game Farm to support his family of five children. He was doing the work of several men so all the children had to get in and do their share before and after school. At a very early age I was milking the cow, turning the separator, getting in the wood, helping in the garden and looking after the horse. We had one horse on the place, a semi-draught — a work horse, not a hack. That's why my father had to do his ranging on a bike.

It was like living in a nature laboratory and I'm not sure whether I inherited or learned from my father the ability to treat sick animals. His constant teaching was: "Look to nature. If you're bright enough it will tell you all the answers."

Running two jobs and doing the work of three men left him little time for reading, even if he'd had the inclination. He read all he needed to know from observing the ways of nature and behaviour of the animals. To his natural gifts he added sound common sense, hard work and patient observation.

Once, when he hatched out pheasant eggs under bantam hens, we learned some interesting facts about pheasants. When the birds were cooped up for breeding, if too many hens were put in with one cock, one of them would undergo a sex change. It would start to grow male plumage and by the next season it could be put in with the hens as a cock. The eggs produced from its matings proved to be fertile and the resulting chicks were normal.

That was education! And it was certainly more enjoyable and rewarding to be out liberating trout into the lakes and streams than going to school. My father reared the fish and fed them up in an earth race, and when they were big enough he released them. I can remember travelling from Napier to Lake Tutira on the back of a truck, going round with a stirrup pump, pumping air into the cans. It wouldn't suit today's traffic officers to have a boy walking about on the back of a truck as it sped down

2

the Devil's Elbow and round the bends to Tutira.

The most celebrated work done on the Game Farm was the breeding and rearing of kiwis, and the best known of the Farm creatures was a kiwi brought in with his leg swinging by the sinews after having been caught in a gin trap. My father amputated the injured leg, nursed the bird and made and fitted a wooden leg for him. He became known as Peg-leg Pete.

As injured female kiwis were brought in the flock was built up and Pete became father of a family. Little was known then about the habits of kiwis, but here they lived in a loving and caring environment and finally an egg was laid and hatched out.

Kiwis hadn't been kept in captivity before this and their care was an experiment. Supplying them with a diet of worms was a headache and the whole family had to go out looking for them. We found the easiest method was to lay wet sacks on the grass at night, go out in the morning, lift the sacks and collect the worms underneath. In recent times the kiwis have been fed with meat pellets laced with vitamins but in those days they wanted worms, and worms they got. They now live in splendour, and help to turn the tourist dollar, in the Nocturnal House on Napier's Marine Parade.

With that first egg, no one knew the incubation period. Both male and female took turns to look after the egg and the male couldn't be induced to leave it. They had reason to be proud of it for it was a big egg — about a third the weight of an adult bird. Day followed day and the kiwis sat on the egg. No one wanted to disturb them by taking it away for testing. Everyone seemed to agree that hatching a kiwi egg was a matter of great importance.

Then, about the 80th day, the egg hatched and the little newcomer was received with great joy all round. A new tourist attraction for Hawke's Bay had been established.

The Game Farm also developed into an animal hospital. Vets were scarce and few people could afford medical bills for their animals anyway. My father made up his own remedies and he rarely lost an animal.

Many of the cats in the district were brought to our

place to be castrated on Sunday mornings. One man wasn't keen on having to hold his cat for the operation. He was given a gumboot and told to put the cat head-down into it and hold it steady, but he didn't like the method. He preferred to put the cat head-first into a sack, leaving out the end to be operated on. Unfortunately, this left the cat free to use tooth and claw from inside the sack and he bit his owner swiftly and strategically. My father's unsympathetic comment was, "Now you know how the cat feels."

Life at home was one long education. We were taught to observe and to draw conclusions from what we saw. When the Game Farm was opened up to visitors we showed them round and explained what was being done. We helped to care for the stock and the sick animals.

After this, school was a disappointment. Perhaps I began to have the first stirrings of awareness about methods of communication, for I came to see that words cannot always be trusted — so many different spellings producing the same sound. Words can be used to lie, to misrepresent facts, to hurt people. Words are dynamite and can create great gaps in understanding. Words are just the code we use for thought patterns. Perhaps the thought patterns were the important thing in communication.

There was no one to explain to me that there are other ways of communicating that are much more effective and sincere than words. At least not then. I had known many animals but I hadn't yet met my real teachers.

I left school at 14. There was no problem in deciding on a career. Necessity decided that. It was just before the Depression, times were hard and any job was a good job. I went to work on a 32-hectare orchard not too far from home and was already expected to do a man's work. After four years on the orchard I was made foreman and my pay went up to 45 shillings a week. On that wage a man could afford to marry, and I knew the girl I wanted.

Everyone in Hawke's Bay has their own story of what happened to them in the 1931 earthquake and my first memory is of a terrified horse who wouldn't leave me alone. I was working at the top of a ladder picking

4

greengages when the 'quake struck. The horse was waiting below in the shafts of a four-wheel trolley used to cart the fruit back to the packing shed. My first thought was to release the horse from the trolley and leave her free to run where she wished but she didn't want to go anywhere. She put her head over my shoulder and wouldn't go away. Wherever I went, she followed, sticking close. I finally got her to the stable, got her harness off and put her in the paddock. My problem then was to get myself out of the paddock. Every time I tried to go through the gate she pushed through with me. She wasn't at all keen to be left alone. Finally I closed the gate from the inside, climbed over it, and rushed off to find out how my family had fared.

I ran all the way home and was relieved to find the house still standing and the family safe. A brick wall had fallen on top of my cherished racing bike (on which I'd won the New Zealand 100-mile championship) so I borrowed another and set off towards Napier to help with the rescue work. I had to carry the bike part of the way over collapsed bridges and broken roads. I met my aunt and cousin who were desperately afraid because they couldn't find their daughter and sister who was a pupil at the Technical College. I left them and went to search for her. I found the college a heap of rubble; the bodies of students were being carried out and laid in a nearby school yard. I was taken to see if I could identify my cousin but, thank God, she wasn't among them.

Later in the day she was safely back with her family. Rescuers in the rubble had heard a faint tapping and had burrowed through the fallen bricks to find her. She'd been on the second floor and had gone into a cupboard. When the 'quake hit it jammed the cupboard door shut and she was trapped inside for about five hours. Fortunately for her, this was one part of Napier not ravaged by fire after the shock.

To get to Pakowhai to see if my fiancee was safe I had to put the bike on my shoulder and scramble along the top of the fallen bridge, but it was worth the struggle to find that she and her family were safe.

Orchard work had come to a halt. There was little point in picking fruit when there was no way of transporting it to its markets. So I went working voluntarily on the repairing of houses. I was fixing the sloping roof of one house on the hill when another severe 'quake came. It nearly threw me off the roof and certainly came close to frightening me to death.

Sally and I were married when we were 19. We borrowed money and bought a house for £350 which we paid off at 12 shillings a week.

In the years in which our family of three, two boys and a girl, were growing up, our place developed into another private game farm. Apart from all the usual animals and birds we had an assortment of wild creatures which had adapted remarkably well to the domestic scene for the sake of a good home.

Bambi was a little fawn whose mother had been shot. She was brought home when only a few days old to be hand reared and she liked to come indoors for company and comfort, given the chance. As she got older she had to be enclosed but was released every evening to go for a run. She'd race out the gate and down the road for about a kilometre, then run back home, turn in at the gate and be ready to settle down.

On one occasion I brought home a goat on a push-bike — no easy task — and two days later she gave birth to twins. She became so tame she'd jump up on a bench in the wash-house and wait to be milked; she gave us a regular three pints a day. The baby goats liked to get into the house and would jump onto the furniture or mantelpiece if not watched.

One of the goats left a visitor thinking he'd suffered a nightmare. He left his car door open when he came inside for a chat. On the car seat was a packet of chocolate and some tobacco. When he came out the old goat had eaten his chocolate, wrapper and all, and was chewing his tobacco with great relish. Directing a stream of abuse at the thief he began to drive off. But the goat was determined to have the last word. She jumped onto the car's carrier and, with her mouth full of tobacco, squinted through the rear window and bleated derisively at her victim.

On that quarter-acre section we had ducks, chickens, goats, pigeons, bees, a possum — and our son Bruce's pet sow. By this time I was working for myself as a contractor — fencing, draining, clearing, logging. In my spare time I did the same thing competitively and became a champion axe-man. I still treated sick animals on the properties on which I was working and it seemed to be accepted that I could relate well to animals and train them easily.

I was slowly coming to understand that mental pictures, not words, were the powerful communicators; that this applied to humans as well as animals; and that the facility seemed to spring into action in an emergency such as a threat to life.

On one occasion when I was tree-felling with my son Don I saw him raise the axe over his head to fell a big branch. I could see what he couldn't — that the branch was holding up a tree and, if he cut it, the whole lot would fall on him. There was no point in shouting as a shout wouldn't have been heard over the noise of the chainsaw, so I "hit" him as hard as I could with the warning thought that if he struck that blow he'd be crushed. He got the message instantly and stopped with the axe poised over his head and a very surprised look on his face. When he came to where I stood he could see what I'd seen and was very thankful he had not struck that blow.

There were occasions when I stopped work and went home because I'd received a mental message from Sally to say that one of the children was ill or hurt. There was also the time when I was at sea and the boat's motor broke down, leaving me drifting in bad weather. Sally got my messages and arranged to send out help.

I was told of an incident in the South Island when a small boy woke up at night, upset and in tears, after what could have been a nightmare. He told his mother that he was thinking about someone who was lost in the bush without food, someone who was old and afraid he was going to die there. The child was so upset that his mother contacted the authorities and was surprised to hear that an

7

elderly man had been missing for two days.

The boy was questioned about his dream and finally said he knew the place. He'd been there on a scouting expedition. His scoutmaster was asked to lead the police to the remote place and there they found the elderly man, cold, hungry and fearful. He was completely bushed, had informed no one of his intentions and would certainly never have been found without the boy's intervention. It seemed certain that in his fear the man had transmitted the plea for help which the boy's mind had picked up like a radio message.

It was happening too often to be coincidence. Slowly I came to accept the fact that mind could communicate directly with mind and that pictures, not words, were the medium.

Being self-employed as a contractor made life easier for the family. It opened up the possibility of a wider life. With the truck it was possible to get to the beach and enjoy nature in a different environment. I discovered the world of the shore line and the off-shore waters, the sea and its ways. And I met the dolphins who were to provide me with the answers to the questions with which I was struggling.

I had spent my life up to this point working with and observing the ways of living things. Now nature was providing me with a whole new laboratory, other creatures to come to know and study.

And I was ready to be taught.

The dolphin —
friend and teacher

I was getting older and bush work seemed to be getting harder, so when the opportunity came to take to the sea for a living, I bought an 8-metre boat and started out as a single-handed commercial fisherman. It was 1954.

Now I was working in the deep water, getting to know the sea and its wonders and I didn't have long to wait to find out what had brought me there. I met the dolphins within a few minutes of leaving port on the first day I sailed — beautiful creatures diving and playing and swooping all round the boat — and they escorted me on my way. The friendliness they displayed astounded me. They seemed as pleased to have my company as I was with theirs. A good dog or a fine horse is a beautiful sight but these sea mammals were something else.

My working days were spent in the company of herds of dolphins for Hawke Bay abounds with them. The underground water aquifers of the Heretaunga Plains flow beneath the coastline and escape into the ocean about 40 kilometres out. These freshwater springs in the ocean are several degrees warmer than the coastal currents and make a pleasant place for a dolphin when it is cold.

When sailing to and from the fishing grounds I had time to join in their entertainment. I raced the boat against them, losing every time; I talked to them and, most of all, I observed everything they did. They were quite different from the terrestrial animals I knew so well. The family pets had been taught various behaviours and had become dependent on human care, but these were creatures of the wild who had known little human contact, for very few humans go out to the sea to meet them where they live. They were more responsive than any animal I'd ever

9

known and were certainly swifter and more confident in their responses.

They made no demands on me; they didn't fear me or appear to want to please me. They wanted my companionship only when it suited them. They'd come to me in the boat and enjoy an encounter or a game, then tire of me and swiftly move away in search of more interesting pursuits. I had to conclude that here in the sea were living creatures superior in intelligence to the finest creatures on land.

For a time I believed that they were responding to the sound of my voice when I hailed them from a distance or spoke to them or even swore at them when they got in the way of the nets, but then I observed something that surprised me. However short a sentence I spoke to them, they started to act upon it before the words were uttered. When I raced the boat against them, even the short word "Go!" was anticipated. They were shooting away before my mind had passed the word to my tongue and my tongue had acted upon the impulse. They appeared to be short-circuiting my thought processes and taking the word directly from my mind. This was the great breakthrough in my understanding of mental communication.

From this time on my life involved endless study and experimentation to try to learn more about this marvellous faculty. In an effort to find out whether it was me or the dolphins who were initiating the communication I asked other people to come out in the boat and enjoy a day with the dolphins. But I noticed through careful observation that, although the dolphins made a small extra response to a few people, in general there was little sign that they were picking up non-verbal messages. From this I assumed that, although all dolphins can communicate by mental image, not all people can. I ask myself why this should be so. Is it a gift given to a few — such as an ear for music, or artistic talents — or is it that most people cannot discipline their thoughts for anything but the verbal process?

I knew that dolphins were originally land mammals who, millions of years ago, took to the sea to survive and whose bodies had evolved into a new shape to cope with a new environment. All former external features were eliminated or withdrawn into the body to provide a streamlined shape for swift passage through the sea. It is possible that a parallel development may have taken place in the dolphin's brain; it may have developed into a sophisticated instrument capable of direct transfer of information.

I spent hours at sea analysing my own thought patterns and trying to understand what was happening, to guess at what it was that created compatibility between me and the dolphins so that thought impulses could pass between us. What wavelengths exist that we could be using if we only knew how? I saw clearly that they could choose to respond or not respond to my thought impulses. If they were busy with feeding or mating behaviour, these being much more important to them than I was, they didn't care about me or my company. I searched out what information I could find about the dolphin sonar system, or echo-location, which serves them so well. I understood that they were producing impulses and transmitting them to objects beyond their vision, and that, they received back echoes which were transmitted to the brain as true images superior to visual images. Sophisticated analysis enabled them to assess the size, shape and texture of an object. And they were using this talent millions of years before computers and video screens were invented.

How can an animal achieve such brain activity which a human being cannot? Have we allowed speech communication to block other forms of communication? Why can some humans transmit mental images to the creatures and not others?

To sum up what the dolphins had taught me thus far — it was clear that I was able to communicate my thoughts to the dolphins and count on them to respond in a friendly way to my own friendly approaches. I could confidently expect them to respond to my requests. I do not use the word command. I knew that they were receiving my mental images and that any words I used — such as "Go" — served only to help me define the mental image I wanted. They were not part of the message.

I was overwhelmed by the vision of what dolphins could do for mankind. We've found the way to make machines that can do what the dolphins do but we've not learned to do it ourselves. Take away the machines and we're helpless. Will we ever learn?

My time as a commercial fisherman was a time of learning, observing and trying to fit the pieces together. The next phase of my life began when it was decided to catch dolphins from the bay and put them on display as a holiday attraction in Napier.

Dolphins on display

At first it seemed an outrageous suggestion to take such beautiful, swift, free creatures and confine them in a pool. Then other considerations began to present themselves. How are people ever to get the opportunity to know dolphins if they remain hidden in the depths of the sea? And if we don't know them how can we ever learn their secrets? Also, there is a simple, shared joy beyond understanding when human meets dolphin and it's certain that humanity would benefit from such encounters.

In most people, dolphins seem to bring out their warmer, kinder, more loving attributes. And certainly dolphins have a great interest in and curiosity about people. I finally came down in favour of taking a few dolphins from the sea when I heard serious discussion on a possible lucrative cat-food industry if permission could be gained to hunt dolphins. Clearly, it was time for the public of New Zealand to get to know the dolphins, to learn to love them and join in a concerted effort to protect them. As a result of this human contact, it is certain that no one in New Zealand today would ever dare to suggest putting dolphins into tins.

If the dolphins were to be caught it was essential that it be done in a way that would not send them into shock, and that they be cared for by people who could establish a good rapport with them and give them a sense of security in their new surroundings. I had no part in the planning. I was simply the fisherman asked to devise a way of catching them, to go out and get them, and then to undertake to supply fish to feed them.

How to catch them was the problem. I have detailed in

a previous book the tail-grab method adopted so will not go into it again. Suffice it to say that my son Bruce and I spent days at sea with stop-watch in hand, timing the dives and surfacing and breathing of the dolphins. We finally decided on a method of catching them by the tail, lifting the head and swinging them on board. I didn't know it, but Jacques Cousteau and his team aboard Calypso were working on the same problem and coming to a similar conclusion. They had the full resources of the French Bureau of Marine Research behind them yet it took them months to achieve what we came up with in a few days and made up in the garage at home. I was working on an expenses-only basis and my main expense was the hiring of two extra crewmen for catching trips so it was possible to land our dolphins at a cost of £40 a time. I wonder what Cousteau cost the French marine authorities?

And so, in early 1965, the first dolphins were caught without any trouble and without sending them into shock. As soon as they were on board they were comforted and reassured and this continued all the way to the pool. Once they reached the pool my part was over and I returned to my own work. Nothing changed in my life for about six months. I had to catch a few months' supply of mullet for the dolphins while the fish was available. It had to be caught, packed and deep-frozen so I fished by night and packed at a local fish-processing plant by day.

No attempt was made to train the dolphins as it was generally believed that the common dolphins of Hawke Bay wouldn't respond to training and would therefore be useless as performers. All overseas film-makers and oceanaria used the bottlenose dolphin, so bottlenose had to be ordered from overseas while the common dolphins were kept like large goldfish for the public to look at. People came to see and admire them but their only "performance" was their willingness to line up and be fed copious amounts of mullet. It wouldn't have surprised me if all these dolphins had died of boredom in their captivity but somehow they held on; perhaps they were curious to see what happened next.

14

To me they were a challenge to test out what I'd learned from my free and easy encounters with dolphins at sea. One night, after I had delivered the next day's fish, I went out to the end of the feeding board and tried to achieve some mental link with the dolphins. All was quiet, the place deserted. Even the city traffic outside had died down; the only spectator was Frank Logan, the pool manager.

I formed in my mind a dolphin's eye view of the scene — underwater, then from surface level, looking up at me standing on the board. The dolphins came and gathered round me — eager, friendly grins on their faces. There was silence, no distractions. I formed an image of the dolphins darting off and swimming round the pool. Even as the thought formed in my mind, they set off round the pool in the direction indicated, then flashed back to me and sat up in the water, waiting for more. My shouts of pleasure seemed to delight them and for who knows how long they swam and jumped and danced in the pool as one image after another formed in my mind. And I jumped and danced and rejoiced on the board with them.

The spell was broken by Mr Logan applauding; I'd forgotten he was there. The upshot of this was that I was appointed head trainer and the training of common dolphins as performers began at once without the use of whistles or food rewards. For the next four years I lived in a privileged observation situation, a university of animal behaviour. I enjoyed working with the sea-lions as well as the dolphins but found that they don't have the mental capacity of dolphins. Being incurably greedy, they worked solely for food rewards.

In dealing with the dolphins I was reminded by the underwater viewing windows that achieving communication demanded that the message be limited to dolphin experience and perception. The message I seemed to get from them was, "Open your mind to our way of thinking — think like a dolphin." I believe I always tried to do this.

From time to time it was necessary for me to try to think like other animals. There was at one time an ill-conceived scheme for including a chimp's tea-party in the Marineland attractions. The chimps were boisterous, and unruly, hard to train and their handler had a difficult time with them. One of them in particular he had to chase all over Marineland; the chase ended with the trainer breathing threats at the foot of the flagpole while the chimp clung to the top of it, sending down on his trainer the ultimate in monkey defence. When the trainer had to be absent for a time I was left in charge of the chimps and found them docile enough.

On another occasion I offered to tie up a police dog while the constable went inside Marineland. The dog-handler told me the dog would eat me if I touched him. When the dog was put in the van I offered to get in with him, but was told the dog would attack anyone who tried. This discussion ended with me sitting in the van stroking the dog while the handler got very angry with his dog for not responding as instructed.

In the close man-dog relationship of the police force, many of the handlers must be practising mental communication with their dogs whether they realise it or not.

Perhaps my most interesting encounter with new animals was with six circus lions. Their trainer and co-performer visited Marineland while the circus was in town. Ringo, one of our performers, was the biggest Californian bull sea-lion I've ever set eyes on and when I asked the circus man if he'd like to come in with me to receive a kiss from Ringo, he declined hastily. "Not on your life," was his reply. "He could bite faster than a snake could strike or a lion use its claws."

I tried to taunt him into accepting but he turned the tables on me by asking if I'd like to come to the circus that evening and accompany him into the lion's cage. I accepted because I'd always wanted to feel the texture of a lion's coat. Within 30 minutes of his departure from Marineland it was all arranged.

There was a full audience under the big top — the appearance of a local in the lion's cage had been well advertised. The audience were asked to keep very quiet and give me a fair go. The six lions waited in their cage. The trainer opened the cage door and went in armed with a whip and chair. He beckoned me in and handed me the whip and chair.

"I don't want either of those and I don't want you in here either."

So he went out and shut the door, leaving me alone. I picked out the biggest lion of the six because he looked like the boss of the pride. I'd discovered with sea-lions that if you can control the boss bull he will control the rest of the animals. I ignored the rest of the pride and concentrated only on the big fellow. I kept my eyes fixed on him and he kept his on me. I moved slowly towards him, knelt down beside him and started to stroke him from his neck down his back, indicating to him with everything I could muster that we were friends. He made no objection to being stroked and after five or six caresses I rose slowly to my feet and backed away from him. I moved to the gate, the trainer opened it and I backed out to the applause of the audience.

The trainer told me afterwards that I couldn't have picked a worse lion as he controlled the rest of them, but this was precisely why I'd chosen him.

Most farmers will tell you that in using dogs to control sheep the farmer must first control the dog, and many of them are doing this by non-verbal communication. When the dog gets the message from the farmer it has no trouble in passing it on to the sheep. Any owner of a trial dog will certify that they can guide the dog when out of visual contact with it, when the dog is perhaps behind a hill and out of whistle contact.

Many trial-dog owners came to me after the Marineland show to say they've never seen such precision in an animal obeying a command and that if they could do the same with their dogs they could win every championship in the world. The dolphin has been working with this method for so long that it has refined it and the immediate response from a dolphin has to be seen to be believed.

I'm certain that members of my family and the

Marineland staff were working with non-verbal communication but they were loath to admit it and preferred to think that their words were the key to the response. Sometimes certain members of the public would have a special attraction for the dolphins; this was often the case with small children. I suspect that such people, without being aware of it, had the habit of thinking in images and that their thoughts were getting through to the dolphins.

I believe that these dolphins were happy, co-operative and healthy because they had friends with whom they could communicate and that they were stimulated by what was requested of them and by the pleasure that came back to them. Had they been left alone with no one to talk to and no audience to applaud them, the transition from freedom to captivity would have been so traumatic that they wouldn't have lived long. As it was, our stable of performers blossomed and made friends with people from all over the world. Visitors responded to their robust humour and they certainly played up to their admirers.

They were still happy and working well when I left Marineland after a disagreement with the board on policy. I felt that some board members were insensitive to the welfare of the dolphins and not prepared to listen to the recommendations of the staff.

On the day I walked out of Marineland for the last time, I vowed that until my death I would never give up fighting for the welfare of those creatures which had become a part of me, a vow which was strengthened by the deaths within a few months of the four dolphins which had been the mainstay of the performance and the source of great pleasure for so many people.

A wild and wayward dolphin

He was 1200 metres from shore, his dorsal fin cutting the water's surface. It was my first sighting of a friend who was to make that summer an interesting and exciting one for me and many other people.

Horace appeared in the waters of Hawke Bay in September 1978. I was giving a series of lectures on cetacea at the Community College at the time and two of my students told me about a lone dolphin they'd spotted at Tangoio, 15 kilometres north of Napier.

As I studied the dolphin's movements through binoculars I wondered if he was just idling for a time in the bay before moving on, or would he stay long enough to enable me to achieve a dream — to study a dolphin not influenced by a man-made environment as at Marineland? Could it be my chance to prove to all that food for reward was unnecessary to get a response from a dolphin?

"Stick around," I urged. "Don't go. Give us a chance to get to know you."

He stayed. It was to be nine months before he left; months of daily observation, painstaking recording and hilarious encounters. He was a three-metre-long bottlenose, and I named him Horace, after Horace Dobbs who'd written a book about a wild dolphin off the English coast.

For the first 10 weeks Horace kept to himself, and few people knew he was there at all. We made no attempt to go out to him. We merely watched and charted his movements.

Satisfying his appetite was Horace's primary concern at this stage. After staying for some weeks in a patch of water 1200 metres from shore, about four kilometres long and one kilometre wide, he began to reconnoitre to the south until, by November, he was abreast of Bay View and only about eight kilometres from Napier Harbour.

Horace made his first friend here. It was a marker buoy, a 25-gallon, heavy plastic drum attached by a chain to an anchor on the sea-bed. The buoy became his base and he always returned to it as soon as the regular chore of satisfying his appetite was completed. He swam round it slowly and endlessly, at a distance of about five metres, seemingly happy in its company.

However, after a time it became obvious that Horace was becoming restive and uneasy. As summer came and the sea's temperature rose, there was an increase in numbers of mullet, a favourite with dolphins. Able to fill himself quickly with little effort, Horace found himself with time to spare. I judged that this was the onset of the danger period for a wild dolphin, when loneliness and boredom could lead him to give up and die. I had made certain deductions about Horace's solitary state and his behaviour was confirming this.

It was a fair guess that Horace had been expelled for showing excessive interest in the females of his own herd. The lifestyle of the Bottlenose dolphin incorporates the habit of expelling from the herd a sexually maturing young male if he is disregarding the laws of the herd regarding sexual activities and is causing a danger of degeneration through inbreeding.

We still have much to learn about these matters and it is only as dolphins allow us to get to know and study them that we will learn. Until the tagging of members of family groups can be carried out we can only guess at the movements of expelled male dolphins in that period between their expulsion and the time when they are mature and strong enough to collect and retain their own females and form a new herd.

Horace's chances of survival would depend on his ability to deal with his daily physical needs, and with the psychological stress of isolation on a gregarious creature.

This was the fascinating dolphin drama we were

observing. Horace had coped with feeding himself and making territorial surveys of his environment. He had tried to satisfy his longing for company by befriending the marker buoy, but it had proved dull company. He was bored and lonely. Craving companionship, he moved closer to Napier and adopted another marker buoy off Westshore Beach, mecca for holidaymakers. Horace had come to town.

After he'd established himself for a time at the Westshore buoy, Horace began to gravitate shorewards. He would approach the beach underwater, come up for a breath and a quick look around, then submerge again. Early one morning he made a cautious approach to my son Bruce but his courage failed him at the last moment. Bruce was operating a drag-net from the beach and Horace followed the cod-end of the net, keeping a close eye on the fish in it. However, as soon as the net was pulled clear of the water onto the beach Horace vanished.

His next approach must have seemed to him less hazardous. If he couldn't yet bring himself to deal with people on the beach, perhaps he could expect more from people who were in his own element, the sea, with him.

There were usually skindivers around the hulk of the wrecked ship Northumberland. The wreck lies off the shingle beach between Bay View and Westshore. Horace discovered that not only was great feeding available at the wreck but there was also human company in his environment where he felt safe and confident.

However, his hopes of social contact were to be dashed. The appearance of such a large creature nosing up to them underwater had a startling effect on the divers. Even when they hit the beach after a record-breaking dash, they were sure the dorsal fin cruising after them belonged to a shark and not a dolphin. Word soon spread that there was an enormous shark patrolling the wreck and in the telling it grew to five metres long and as big around the girth as an elephant.

For quite some time the wreck was deserted.

I was certain that Horace's craving for companionship was approaching crisis point and would soon override his natural caution. I felt great sadness and compassion for this solitary creature. He was the victim of his own male nature and the law of his species by which an individual must be sacrificed to the welfare of the species as a whole. He was just a young thing away from his own kind and very lonely in this strange place. His craving for companionship had brought him to the town beaches and the people. Even so, any relationship must be on his own terms; it must not be forced upon him. It was now December and I waited for his invitation.

His next move was an overture to the surf life-saving boat and its crew. He hovered around them when they went out on their evening training. Was it chance or dolphin know-how that made him choose this boat and its crew? Did he sense that these people, surely, wouldn't harm him? Horace followed the boat on several evenings.

Then, one evening he approached and made overtures to a fisherman in a dinghy. The excited fisherman rang me and described the incident. The dolphin had sped round and round the boat, squeaking and jabbering.

"I know you'll think I'm crazy," said the fisherman, "but I'm sure he was asking me to race with him."

These friendly encounters gave Horace the boost he needed. That same evening he put on a magnificent display of leaping, splashing and tail-walking round his buoy. Those of us watching from shore agreed the display would have done credit to a Marineland performer.

It was the invitation we'd been waiting for. Horace had come out of hiding. He was throwing all his tricks into a great big public announcement of his presence and his availability for friendly approaches.

Horace meets the people

That night I couldn't sleep. I was longing to get out there to Horace and lay awake wondering how it could be done. I no longer owned a boat but was determined that, one way or another, I was going to get out to him.

The story of Horace's performance had spread overnight, and next morning a TV cameraman was waiting to join me in a boat I'd borrowed. We were joined by David Wheeler, a freelance photographer and long-time helper. We headed out to the buoy and suddenly saw a body streaking through the water towards us, clearing some of the waves, ploughing through others. Horace! As he drew near he went up in the air in a leap five metres high. He landed on his side with a resounding splash, then went up again even higher. The others were entranced but both Bruce and I took the opportunity to confirm that he was indeed a male.

Bruce and a friend went quietly over the side and Horace swam slowly towards them. While they trod water, he swam between them. He taunted them into chasing him but wouldn't allow them to touch his tail flukes. Bruce finally caught hold of his dorsal and was towed along in the water. As soon as Horace escaped from his grasp he performed a sideways tailwalk, something I've never seen at Marineland.

The light was fading and the swimmers were tired. Not so Horace. As we turned to go back to port he came alongside the boat and lifted the forward part of his body out of the water as though to say, "Don't go." We left him with regret.

David Wheeler's pictures appeared on the front page of

next evening's newspaper. Horace had gone public.

Now that our relationship had become closer, the watch on Horace would need to be constant. I tried to work out a budget that would make the best use of our limited funds, and I found it a depressing exercise. I was sitting at the table in the kitchen window, looking out through the spreading fronds of a tree-fern, past the lemon trees and the grapefruit trees to the gate. A Land-Rover, with a boat in tow, stopped outside. Bruce got out of the cab and I went out to meet him.

"Well, how do you like her?"

I walked round the boat and inspected it. I liked what I saw.

"Where did you borrow this?"

"I didn't. It's mine."

So it was back inside to the kitchen table and on with the kettle while we heard the story. He'd bought the boat and trailer on time payments and swapped his car for the Land-Rover. Bruce had worked with me at Marineland as a dolphin trainer; he was the striker in my three-man catching team. Since our resignation from Marineland he'd worked on the wharf, but always managed to be available to help me at whale strandings or any other service in the study of marine mammals. He insisted that he'd bought the boat because he wanted to get in some fishing, but he later admitted to his mother that it was to give me the opportunity to learn all Horace had to teach about inter-species thought transference. What better companion could one wish for in the Horace experiment?

"Want to try her out?"

Did I? Lunch was just about on the table but we left it and drove off to what was to be a very beautiful encounter with Horace. He came to meet us in a swift, direct dash from the buoy, executing a series of jumps close to the boat without causing a splash or a ripple — poetry in motion. The sea all around us was calm and tranquil. It was a moment of great peace and harmony. Horace came alongside the boat and Bruce and I spoke quietly to him, expressing our deeply-felt admiration for his beauty. Although the words could mean nothing to him he

The author with his
parents and sisters,
photographed in 1922.

The author winning the
40-mile Hawkes
Bay/Poverty Bay senior
cycling championships in
1931.

"My working days were
spent in the company of
herds of dolphins . . ."
Rare shot of common
dolphins mating.

Daphne, the first dolphin caught for Marineland, being transported to the dolphin pool.

This newborn calf at Marineland unfortunately didn't survive beyond four months.

The author's daughter Brenda with her namesake – Brenda the dolphin.

Horace. Quentin Bennett

As Horace became bored and lonely, he gravitated towards Westshore Beach, where there was usually some sort of action near shore.

Horace exhibiting weird behaviour.

Horace tailwalking backwards for Bruce Robson and a companion close inshore at Westshore Beach.

Horace playing "seaweed games" with a swimmer. The scratch marks on his body indicate the reason for his separation from his family group.

Horace brought this piece of seaweed to the surface, draping it over his flipper in response to the author's mental request. Note the reaction of the woman at left: she'd asked me to get him to do this and was astonished at the result!

certainly took their meaning. He lay on the water, sleek and beautiful and quiet, and accepted our admiration in an atmosphere of calm sea, happy dolphin and entranced humans.

When his busy mind had had enough of this harmony, he made an inspection of the boat. He gave the shaft and propeller a good survey and we put the motor gently into gear to satisfy his curiosity. Then he was ready for some fun — to challenge the boat. He shot from behind to a position a few metres in front and began to cavort in an inviting manner that was familiar to me. I have many times seen dolphins in the sea offer this challenge and I have many times accepted it. I have never yet won such a race. Without either of us speaking, Bruce reached gently for the throttle. Horace couldn't see the move but before the hand reached the throttle, the race was on and he took off in a straight line. Over and over he was to respond to thought impulses without a word being spoken.

Finally we told him we were going home. Again the word meant nothing but the picture in our minds of the boat entering the harbour did. Before Bruce had time to turn the wheel Horace was streaking ahead in a straight course into the harbour. It was clear that in him we had an excellent subject for studies into thought transference. It was also clear that in his own environment he was our superior by far and not in any danger from boats cruising at reasonable speeds. He could attain speeds of up to 35 knots for 400 metres before breaking off and veering sharply to left or right. He could maintain 12 knots for very long periods. The speed at which he left the water, executing high jumps of up to seven metres, must have been phenomenal to propel his body weight — an estimated 230 kilograms — to such a height.

Bruce and I made our plans for the Horace watch. Bruce took a few weeks' leave to act as skipper and diver. Large numbers of people were now anxious to get out to the buoy and it became the busiest spot in the bay. We took many people out but larger groups began to charter the larger game-fishing boats for trips to the buoy and the favourite resident of the bay.

My wife had little time to spend with Horace. She undertook to answer the phone and deal with people making enquiries or reporting what they'd seen. During those weeks of December we missed many meals and much sleep but we kept close to Horace and improved our acquaintance with him.

I'm happy to say that the public of Hawke Bay took a childlike pleasure in Horace's company and seemed united in a determination to care for him. I would have been sorry for anyone caught troubling him. However, I felt that some way of instructing and also reassuring the public was necessary (many people still believed a shark had taken up residence at Westshore). I discussed it with Ian Johnson, student at the Community College, and he undertook to get out a brochure. With some financial help from the Napier City Council, the Community College printed 3000 brochures. These were distributed free to residents and holidaymakers. Many of these excellent brochures have since found their way round the world.

The brochure gave information about dolphins in general and about those on the New Zealand coast in particular. It gave advice on how to behave towards Horace and how to know the difference between him and a shark.

It promised — "Look after Horace and you will be part of a rare experience."

The rare experience was already under way. Horace seemed to be exercising a beneficial effect upon people. Members of the public, residents, holiday visitors, fishermen, boaties, divers and swimmers — all seemed united in a pact to ensure Horace's safety. And nobody was making any money out of the situation.

In a previous book, I have discussed the widely held belief that dolphins are a benevolent influence in the world. This is recorded in ancient history and it is found in oral history and legends passed down. Maori people are among many cultures who hold to this belief. However, it also seems to be a truth of this world that a good and loving influence is always under attack from the darker powers. Art and literature use this theme again and again.

26

Dolphins generate great love and friendship but they have also been the subject of savage cruelty.

An interesting feature of the Community College brochure was an account of the dolphin in local Maori legend. It was contributed by Te Rina Sullivan-Meads. She wrote:

"Horace is not the first dolphin to befriend people in the seawaters off Ahuriri (Napier) for, just as dolphins abound in Greek and Roman legend and art, so, too, they figure strongly in the Maori legends of the Hawke Bay area.

"It is told that when Takitimu, the ancestral canoe of the Ngati Kahungunu people of Hawke Bay, voyaged from Hawaiiki to New Zealand, it was frequently escorted by dolphins. After its arrival in New Zealand waters, Takitimu made a number of landings around the North Island. One such landing took place near Napier.

"In time the Ngati Kahungunu people established themselves on the shores of the lagoon which is now the Inner Harbour. The dolphins were the frequent companions of the people as they gathered the abundant sea-foods in the lagoon and along the coast. On many occasions children and dolphins befriended one another.

"For the ancient Maori, and those who still nurture the ancient knowledge today, the dolphin is their aumakua or katikati, their protection relation, their family member in the sea, their sign of good luck and safety.

"One event that shows the spiritual affinity between Maori and dolphin is recorded in a lament. The lament tells of a battle many years ago when the Ngati Kahungunu suffered defeat at the hands of the tribes of Hauraki.

"A young boy's body was pulled from the sea at Ahuriri and ceremonially eaten by the victorious leader and his men. The boy was high-born and in him was the mana of his people. A guardian spirit living in the

27

sea near the coast of Ahuriri took the form of a dolphin and became the boy's spiritual guardian. The spirit was believed to be the manifestation of an early ancestor, one of those who landed from the ancestral canoe at Ahuriri. The guardian spirit in the form of a living dolphin is believed to be in the sea near Ahuriri."

A modern Maori attitude was expressed by another Maori friend whose husband took Bruce and me out in his boat to Horace. This is her story:

"When my husband went out with Frank and Bruce that night, I put a blessing on them. I stood on the beach and put a blessing on them. They didn't know it but I did.

"I knew those fellows wouldn't hurt a dolphin but there were other boats and divers out there and I didn't know if all those people could be trusted. They might do something bad to the dolphin and I didn't want our boys mixed up in anything bad that might happen then.

"Me, I have mixed feelings about that dolphin. A dolphin is a sign — a tohu. But a sign of what? I don't know yet whether this one is a good or a bad sign. I suppose it depends on the people and what they make of it.

"I heard about the dolphin from my husband. He came home from fishing. He was cleaning his gear. He said, 'We've got a mate out there, a dolphin. He keeps nosing around and diving and playing with us.'

"I said, 'How do you feel about it? Have you got any funny feelings about it?'

'No. Why should I?'

'You know that dolphin is a tohu, a sign?'

'A sign of what? You tell me that.'

'I couldn't tell him. I didn't know.'

"But I do know that Maoris have a special affinity with dolphins. Maoris are fishermen and dolphins are friends of fishermen. My old ones and my own father have all been fishermen. If they were out in a boat and they saw a dolphin they always treated it with respect.

They never took a dolphin for granted just like anything else that swims in the sea. They knew it was the sign of the protection of their ancestors. They knew it was a tohu.

"I knew a man up north. He was diving for kinas (sea-eggs) commercially. He came in from one of the islands and sat down to eat with us. He said he'd been coming in in his boat and he saw dolphins alongside. He got one. I couldn't believe what he was saying.

'Don't tell me you speared it?' He nodded.

'I did. And I pulled it alongside my boat.'

'Didn't you know better than that? Didn't your elders tell you about dolphins.'

'No.'

'They didn't tell you that we have to look after them because they look after us?'

'No. I never heard that. We lived in the bush most of our lives. We didn't know much about the sea then.'

"I said, 'Just the same, your old ones should have taught you properly and not let you grow up ignorant about these things. You've done a terrible thing.'

"A few days later he was coming in again in his boat. He was coming over the river bar. Everything was perfectly calm. Then his boat just overturned and he lost all his gear and his food and everything in the boat. He was lucky that was all he lost.

"I asked my husband again, 'Have you thought about your feelings towards that dolphin?'

"He said, 'Look, I'm just glad we've got a mate out there.'

'All right then,' I said. 'You just see that no one does anything to that dolphin. You tell them all that it isn't safe to mess around with that dolphin.'

In the days before Christmas Bruce and I took many visitors out to see Horace at the buoy and they were all amazed at the warm reception he gave. One of my visitors, Tom Lowry of Okawa thoroughbred stud fame, summed up his admiration for the big dolphin with the comment, "He's as big as a bull but much more elegant."

Horace began to perform at regular times and even people without a boat knew what time to gather on the Esplanade to watch. His usual times were between 7.30 and 8.30 in the mornings and 6 and 8 in the evenings.

We were into the fine summer evenings and whole families took to having al fresco meals at Westshore. Sometimes there was almost a traffic jam on the Esplanade when he was performing well. One evening I counted 250 cars parked facing seawards. Some of the occupants believed they could attract Horace into action by flashing their car lights on and off. Viewed from the sea they were quite a spectacle.

I found myself in the line of fire of two groups of people and I sympathised with the views of both. One group wanted me to bring Horace in close to the beach so everyone could enjoy him, not just boat-owners. The other wanted me to ensure he stayed in safely where he was because they feared he might be harassed or even shot at if he came right in to the beach.

I could only tell them that Horace would make his own decisions and that no one was going to put any pressure on him. When we were with Horace and decided to go elsewhere, we simply told him where we were going. Frequently he would set off ahead of us in the direction mentioned. I repeat that he was not responding to the words — how could he? He was responding to a mental image. Many times we stopped for a short talk with him when we were on our way elsewhere. If we were going to the wreck to dive for mussels we'd ask him if he was coming with us. Although we used words because this is our main method of communication, Horace responded to a mental picture of the wreck, an underwater picture, a Horace-eye view of the wreck. When this picture was consciously transmitted to him, he would often shoot straight off in the direction of the wreck.

We were careful always to obey the rule about allowing him to feed in peace. Sometimes we waited politely for him to finish. He wouldn't hurry with his meal but would be sociable about it by bringing an occasional fish to the boat to show us before he ate it.Horace appeared so relaxed that it was sometimes easy to forget that he had other needs, needs that we were powerless to fulfil.

The 'squeaky door' and other sounds

Just before Christmas Horace began a new behaviour. After showing off some of his aerobatic feats one night he approached the marker buoy. The buoy is of heavy plastic construction, the type of container in which acids are transported. It was anchored by a chain to a block of concrete and stood upright about a metre above the surface of the water. The dolphin lifted his body up above the buoy and then allowed his weight to push down on it. His flippers helped to stabilise his weight until he'd pushed the buoy about halfway down. Then its buoyancy tipped him off to one side. He fell into the water and the buoy bobbed up again. He tried again. And again, sometimes sliding off sideways, sometimes head-first.

After many attempts he had some success, provided he kept moving and let the buoy slide along his underside for the entire length of his body. However, most of his efforts were fruitless and after 20 minutes he got bored and went off to follow a boat. At the time I wasn't sure whether this was just play or whether it was sexual behaviour. A few days later we were able to prove to our satisfaction that it was indeed sexual behaviour.

We'd come to suspect that certain sounds aroused Horace and linked this with his behaviour towards the marker buoy when we noted that he only demonstrated this behaviour when the sea was choppy. We waited for such a day and then went out to the buoy to carry out experiments. Bruce put on a weightbelt to help him remain submerged and went overboard beside the buoy to find out what sounds Horace could hear underwater. I used a home-made listening device in the boat. We both heard the sound.

It was the action of the large-link chain which attached the buoy to its anchor. When the links moved against one another in a choppy sea they gave off what we came to call the 'squeaky door' sound. When a choppy sea tossed the buoy about and caused the links to move and squeak, Horace responded as he would to the inviting squeaks of a female dolphin. He never responded sexually unless he was given the green light and it soon became clear that the squeaky door sound was the green light.

Some time later we tried a further experiment with sound. While underwater, Bruce imitated a squeaky-door sound as well as he could, and was charged by a very excited Horace. Bruce saw him coming in time to get out of the way by springing onto the stern-step of the boat. He made up his mind there and then never to make that sound underwater again.

"He sure meant business that time," he said as he clambered into the boat.

"It's a good job you weren't wearing lipstick," I said, "or he might have tried to get into the boat with you."

The rare occasions when Horace was rough with his friends could be attributed, I believe, to touches or sounds that caused sexual arousal. When Horace played so happily and amiably it was hard for people to remember that he was a strong young male animal. One would be wary with a young entire horse or a bull, and one would not expect a tom-cat always to play like a kitten. On the rare times when Horace butted his friends in the ribs or nipped them on the backside, I believe this was caused by frustration after swimmers in the water with him had been stroking his underside with hands or feet, just as the female dolphin strokes the male with her flippers.

In contrast to the effects of the squeaky door sound, we soon discovered that a good hearty laugh underwater through a snorkel had a most benign effect on the dolphin. One day Quentin Bennett, a noted underwater photographer, came out with us to get some pictures. Bruce and Dave were diving with him that day. Horace swam straight up to Quentin and looked in through his face-mask. Quentin began to laugh through the snorkel, and this had a most remarkable effect on Horace. He began to jabber at Quentin and nudge his hand. His mouth was slightly open and Quentin rubbed his beak gently. Horace opened his mouth wide, revealing a healthy set of teeth. He moved slowly past Quentin, who took hold of the leading edge of the dorsal fin and was towed along for about 10 metres before he let go. Horace made no attempt to dive or to break the hold. Quentin had an appointment to keep and reluctantly tried to end the interlude. He held his hand out to Horace in a farewell gesture. The dolphin moved slowly forward, took the hand in his mouth, then moved slowly round in a circle, towing Quentin by the hand. When he let go he allowed the hand to make contact with the full length of his body as he moved slowly past.

We witnessed an interesting response by Horace on 23 December when a herd of 25 common dolphins approached the buoy as they crossed the bay. Horace bore down on them and put them to flight in no uncertain manner. I wasn't close enough to hear, but I could imagine the guttural sounds he'd be making. His territory had been intruded upon and he wasn't going to put up with it.

Was Horace's behaviour due to the fact that they were common dolphins and not of his species? Was it just a male territorial claim? Had he come to prefer human company, with its attendant adulation? So many questions to be answered, and who knew how long he would stay around to provide the answers?

Horace wasn't forgotten on Christmas Day, either. Thinking he might be lonely we went out to see him. He was in fine form, leaping eight metres into the air again and again. When we left him he was successfully convincing some men in a launch that he was more fun than fishing.

The next day we decided on a new experiment. So far no one had swum with Horace while wearing an aqualung and we wanted to observe his reaction to the bubbles. Two swimmers went in with him wearing wetsuits, face-masks and snorkels. They swam around a bit then came back on board, fitted the aqualungs and went in again. Horace showed no fear of this odd set-up and was in fact very interested. He faced one diver and approached closer and closer until his beak almost touched the glass of the mask. Then he slowly turned his head and looked the diver straight in the eye. The diver carefully stretched out his arms and Horace backed slowly away from the reaching hands. When the diver lowered his arms the dolphin advanced again, to within 15 centimetres of the face-mask, and had another peek through the glass.

It seemed we could do almost anything just so long as we observed his rules and never tried to overstep the limits he'd set.

Rudder shudders

The day came when Horace took the big step of following a yacht through the heads and into the inner harbour, site of a whaling station last century. He went up to the boat moorings and found a new world.

From that day on he spent much time amongst the moored boats and with their crews as they worked on their craft. The boat club premises and fishing vessel wharves won a new popularity as residents and visitors took their strolls and looked out for the dolphin. Patrons at the tavern could sit at their tables and enjoy their beer while watching Horace play and perform.

January is the month of yacht races, regattas and championships, and Horace had a field day among yachts large and small. When a race was being sailed he could usually be found out in front of the leading yacht. If that boat was overtaken he transferred to the bow of the new leader. When the wind was fresh and the boats flew, Horace led the way. When the sails hung limp from a lack of wind and the yachts had to be towed slowly home, Horace meandered in slowly too — but still always in front.

Not all crews were happy about his activities, especially when he took to hampering manoeuvres during a race by leaning his weight against the rudder or, worse, playing with the centreboard and making the yacht veer about.

In one incident a trailer-sailer motoring into port suddenly had its rudder jolted up. A crewman pushed it down again, only to have it thrust back up in his face. His perplexed look was something to behold. When told Horace was the culprit he refused to believe it. Can't be, he assured us. The propeller was too close to the rudder. The dolphin couldn't possibly get so close to the whirling blades. To prove it was Horace I suggested that the crewman push the rudder down gently. He did. Up it came gently. Push it down in two stages. It bounced back in two stages. Ram it down hard. Up it came hard — so hard that it almost flew clear of the casing.

I was from the start a little fearful about Horace's relationship with the fishermen. The day's fishing may be great fun to a dolphin but it is bread and butter to fishermen and they could hardly be blamed for objecting if Horace did anything to interfere with their livelihood.

As things turned out, I didn't need to worry. Horace quickly got the message that the beach fishermen wanted no help from him. He knew that when nets were being lifted fishermen were in no mood for play. He stayed with them and chased the odd escaping fish but he did nothing to interfere with their catch. He made friends with their boats and tended to follow them wherever they went. This increased his territory but it decreased his availability. Sometimes he was nowhere to be found and it would later be reported that he'd followed a boat out and home again on a day-long trip, or that he'd spent hours with a trawler as it worked. He had come a long way from the timid dolphin who stayed close to the marker buoy, his only friend.

The speedboat races were a source of anxiety to many of Horace's friends, and steps were taken to ensure that he had company in a safe place while they were in progress. With people in the water willing to play his games he paid no heed to the screaming engines.

One of his new games was to drape himself with seaweed, show it off to his human friends and then 'lose' it. When asked, "Where's the seaweed?" he'd go off and return with it around his flipper, his dorsal fin or his tail flukes. He was happy to play this seaweed game for as long as swimmers were energetic enough to flounder about in his wake trying to get it off him.

Horace had interesting encounters with many boats but the one he really fell for was a keeler named Tiny Dancer, which was moored close to a beach in the inner harbour. He latched onto her when his marker buoy was removed, depriving him of his 'mate'. He could be found every day pushing violently at her rudder and moving the boat back and forth on her mooring. His tactics got so rough that the yacht's owner lashed the tiller in an effort to stop Horace breaking the rudder from its mountings. I've no doubt that he was attracted to this yacht by the sounds made by her moving rudder, and frustrated by a lack of fulfilment when he responded to her apparent enticements.

Alarms and hazards

During Horace's stay with us there was always a lurking fear that some harm would befall him, and the bolder he got the greater the fear.

The first threat to him came from the danger of being mistaken for a shark and dealt with accordingly. There isn't any doubt about it, a dorsal fin in the water does have a startling effect on people.

When Horace picked Westshore for his headquarters he chose a place where there was always a certain danger from gill netting which is concentrated in the shallow waters of Westshore in the summer months. One evening I counted as many as 26 gill nets. During his early days at the beach, Horace contented himself with watching the nets being shot away in the evening and being on hand in the morning to watch them being picked up.

The nets are set and picked up with a small rowboat and Horace began to make a nuisance of himself by getting into such a position that the oarsman couldn't row in a straight line, an essential to the effective use of a set net. On one occasion Horace found himself inside a drag-net and he wasted no time in getting out over the cork line, and after that he took care to stay behind the net. All these occasions on which Horace made a nuisance of himself increased our worry for his safety.

Horace's admirers always kept a close eye on his wellbeing. I was sometimes contacted by worried people who thought he might be in danger for one reason or another. On several occasions I broke the speed limit from Taradale to Napier on "errands of mercy" that turned out to be false alarms, for which I was thankful.

The only real injury Horace received during his stay

was a one-in-a-million piece of bad luck. We found him one day with five bleeding vertical grooves along his side. We heard from a yachtie that the injury had been sustained in the main harbour area, and we concluded that he'd been hit by a heavy hawser tightening during the berthing of a large ship. Within four days the wounds were healed and Horace enjoyed having the marks rubbed by willing fingers. In a short time it was impossible to see where the wounds had been.

This incident made us aware that Horace was now frequenting the main harbour and was exposing himself to a very real danger in doing so. The Harbour Board was currently engaged on a programme of underwater blasting to deepen the turning basin. The rocky bottom was being blasted and the spoil picked up by suction dredge to be deposited at sea. The work was done by drilling holes in the rock floor and charging them with gelignite. They were primed for explosion at definite times, usually 12 noon and 5 p.m. Warning regulations were strictly adhered to so that no person was in danger but no regulations could ensure that a nosy dolphin would not be around at the wrong time.

Horace had been pleased when he first found his way to the drilling sites. Here he could find skindivers in the water at any time, and divers had always been his favourite humans. The divers were friendly enough when they got used to him although one of them complained to me that he nearly had a heart attack every time this bloody great bullock loomed up in the murky water alongside him.

At first the divers thought it was a good joke when Horace managed to pull a flipper from a diver's foot. It was less funny when he took it more than a few metres away from them and let it drop to the bottom before they could get it back. While they went down to try to retrieve it he swam behind them and tugged off the other flipper. They settled this by strapping on their flippers tightly and Horace had to think up other ways of having fun with the divers. One day I had a phone call from one of the explosives experts.

40

"Will you come and take this dolphin away? He's just a bloody nuisance."

Bruce and I went out in the boat and we told the divers we'd come to remove him as requested. They didn't want him to go.

"Yes," they agreed. "He is a bloody nuisance, but he's a nice bloody nuisance."

We took the opportunity to discuss with them the danger to Horace of their blasting and we asked them to notify us before every blast so that we could ensure that Horace was safely out of the blasting area. A few days later we were advised that a blast would take place at 5 p.m. the next day.

We started looking at 3 p.m. and found him busy with the divers who were priming the shots. They certainly didn't want his company right then because, as they set the primers, he was having a good game trying to pull them out.

"Take him to hell out of it," was their urgent request.

They found it hard to believe that he would go to the inner harbour on our request and that the request would simply be a mental picture of the inner harbour. We had him safely in the inner harbour by 4.30 p.m. and gave him a motor-car tyre to play with. At 5.05 we heard the blast. It was all over and Horace was free to go where he liked.

During the following weeks, this operation became a twice-weekly chore and on every occasion we located him and got him into the boat harbour before blast-off.

The last blast of the programme was scheduled for 5 p.m. but in fact didn't go off until 11 p.m. Everything went wrong that day. Bruce's boat had overheated its motor and there was some delay in getting parts to repair it. Luckily a friend offered us the use of his boat and we located Horace and got him into the Iron Pot anchorage. We kept him amused but we didn't hear the blast and we stayed with Horace until nearly dark. Then we concluded that we'd simply not heard it, so we trailered the boat and went home, leaving Horace to his own devices.

At 11 p.m. people living near the port were awakened by a blast which shook their houses. We learned the next day that the blast had been postponed because of the close proximity of a berthed ship. The ship had sailed at 10 p.m. and by 11 p.m. all was clear and the blast went ahead.

No one could guess where Horace had been at 11 p.m. and during the hours which followed while we searched for him and all the binoculars scanned the sea, we were all very distressed. At 5 p.m. next day our prayers were answered. He appeared at the entrance to the inner harbour on cue as though he was expecting the 5 o'clock blast. The wintry dusk was upon us so we only had time to say hello and goodbye.

On the following afternoon he was in the inner harbour and swimmers and divers played with him. They were not to know that it was for the last time. From that evening, at dusk on 26 May, 1979, Horace was not seen again.

Some people were sure he must have been injured in the late-night blast but he had been seen afterwards, looking lively and playful. If he had died his body would certainly have been washed ashore.

His departure didn't take me by surprise. I had been expecting it for weeks. For some time he'd been getting very fat; this is common in dolphins when the water temperatures drop after the first cold snap which follows the arrival of the first snow on the inland ranges, the onset of winter. We'd had the first snowfall and the temperatures of the inshore waters of the bay had dropped by three and a half degrees. When that happened I knew that Horace would not stay with us much longer.

I made enquiries among the fishermen and was told that on Sunday, 27 May, the day Horace disappeared, they had seen a herd of about 40 Bottlenose dolphins crossing the bay and heading north towards warmer waters. This migrating herd would probably allow another dolphin to tag along with them.

There were many sad people in Hawke Bay in the following weeks. The sea was constantly scanned for a sight of that familiar fin; there were some hopeful false alarms but there was no Horace.

The long and remarkable summer with Horace was over.

And so to Japan

My summer with Horace was interrupted for a few weeks while I went to Japan. My trip was sponsored by the Earth Co-existence organisation of Hawaii and the purpose was the same as that of my project at home — to communicate, without words, this time with another culture rather than another species. We were going to meet and film the Japanese fishermen who annually slaughter thousands of dolphin.

On the Sydney-Japan flight there were only four European travellers so there was not much communicating going on. We landed at Narida airport and there I ran into my first communication difficulty. It would have been easier to talk to a dolphin. I was first up to the immigration counter and the last to get past it as I had great difficulty in explaining the purpose of my visit. On the immigration form I had used the word cetacea; the officer read it, turned it round, pointed to the word and shook his head. I altered it to read whales and dolphins but he shook his head again and I kept changing it until the form was unreadable. I took a form from his desk and drew a picture of a dolphin on it and then he understood. By that time everyone else had gone through so he filled in my card and allowed me to proceed. Communication at that point was not going very well.

At Customs I thought I would fly through as I had only one suitcase while everyone else had trolley-loads of luggage but I was mistaken. After reading my immigration card very carefully, the officer searched my case most thoroughly and found, hidden in amongst my clothing, a packet of my books. He picked the parcel up gingerly and asked, "What is this?"

"It's books."

He obviously didn't believe me. I think he thought it was something dangerous for he opened it very carefully. He stared at the dust cover of the book, a picture of me with my face puckered up to be kissed by a dolphin. Then his face broke into a delighted smile. He pointed at me, he pointed at the picture. Everything was all right but he still took a good look through the books. Then he packed everything neatly, closed the case and with a gracious smile put it on the conveyor and motioned me to pass through. Everyone else had long since gone.

So much for my first effort at mental communication with people of a different culture. I made my way through the maze of escalators and found the exit where I waited to be collected by Dexter Cate, the president of the organisation sponsoring my trip. In the following year he was to achieve worldwide publicity when he cut the net at the dolphin drive and allowed many dolphins to escape. For his effort he spent three months in prison and perhaps was lucky to be then deported from Japan.

That was all in the future; at this stage he was still trying to influence Japanese thinking by diplomatic methods. He was easily recognisable when he came for he stood head and shoulders over most Japanese. His long hair was tied back with a head-band and he was heavily bearded. We had plenty of time to get to know each other on the two-hour drive from the airport into Tokyo.

When we got into the city I found myself taking part in a marathon walking race with this young American whose stride was twice as long as mine. Not only was I handicapped by this and 40 more years of living on this earth but I also had my suitcase to carry and it got heavier and heavier as we charged along. We eventually reached Tokyo University and my pacer shot off the street and into a maze of passages while I laboured along behind him.

Finally, Dexter flung open a door and we were in a room littered with heaps of correspondence. I was introduced to a quiet young woman called Michi who was the Greenpeace co-ordinator in Tokyo.

I just had time to sit down and draw a breath while phone calls were made and then the marathon was on

44

again and this time Michi was striding away ahead of me. It was clear that she was in practice and in good form for walking.

At the first doorway I got my first lesson in the ways of Women's Lib. I stood aside to let Michi precede me and she did not like it so she stood aside also. I motioned to her to go first and she told me very clearly that she did not like this kind of treatment as she considered us equals. I didn't feel equal to anybody at that stage so I went through first, looking contrite at having offended.

When we later got on to public transport I understood her attitude. Chivalry was non-existent and it was every man for himself and every woman for herself. If your backside was unlucky enough to be beyond the line of the automatic doors when they closed there could well be cheap meat for sale. I learned to move very fast and concentrate on my own safety because when the human mass was on the move there was no quarter for anybody.

My case got heavier and heavier and, in spite of my lesson in equality, I refrained from asking Michi to carry it for a while. I didn't feel so inhibited about asking Dexter. He carried it until the weight had stretched his arms an inch or two and then he hoisted it on to his head. He walked in front of our little file and on a number of occasions the case crashed into a low verandah. This would make him stop suddenly and Michi and I would run into him. Then the procession would reform and we would charge on.

After what seemed like the world's longest and hardest trek we arrived at our destination. It had been lent to Dexter by Japanese naturalists in sympathy with his aims. It was their meeting room but they allowed him to live there.

It was a one-room flat in the Japanese style. There were no chairs and the only piece of furniture was a low table. At bedtime, mattresses and covers were taken from a cupboard and laid on the floor and that was the bedroom. In the morning they were put back into the cupboard and that was the living room and dining room back again. Meals were very simple — eggs, milk, fruit and boiled rice which took little time to prepare and little time to eat. Dexter had made a booking for me at a hotel but I was happy to accept the hospitality of the naturalists and not go one step further. Next morning we were up early and on the street again on the way to Marineland, an attraction I was eager to see and to compare with Napier's Marineland.

It was 25 minutes' walk to the station and we were four and a half hours on the train. When we got to Marineland we found two TV crews and radio and press interviewers waiting for us. Everyone seemed to know Dexter and he spoke a little Japanese. Lunch was a treat — a real European meal. We were shown over the complex which is beautifully situated beside the sea. We watched the show and found it very good. The manager gave us two trainers to escort us and take us wherever we wanted to go. My main interest was to get closer to the dolphins and observe their reaction to someone they had never seen and who could not speak to them in words they had ever heard.

Until this time the media reaction had been quiet. If pictures were taken it was done unobtrusively. They had obviously heard about me and my views on non-verbal communication because when I approached the pool they swarmed around me. Microphones on long leads appeared from everywhere and were pointed at me and around me from every possible angle and in every possible place. When I leaned over the pool they crowded close and pushed one another about.

I asked the interpreter to explain that I would not speak or make gestures to the dolphins. I knew not one word of Japanese anyway and the only words of training they would have heard would have been in that language. Through the interpreter I told them what I was asking the dolphins to do. First I would ask them to roll over. The interpreter told them this. There was silence. Then the dolphins rolled over. I said I would ask them to come and shake hands with me. They came up and took my hand in their mouths. I think the Japanese were surprised at the result and they discussed it eagerly amongst themselves.

I was then taken to a pool which had been set up as an experiment to encourage dolphins to breed in captivity and produce more dolphins for the establishment. In it were three adult dolphins, the biggest I had ever seen of their species — one male and two females. They had been in isolation in this pool for two years and had not been exposed to training in any way. They were kept separate from the other dolphins and the staff were forbidden to have any contact with them apart from feeding and normal care. The idea was to keep them in a situation similar to their world in the sea and hope they would then reproduce.

The experiment had had no success so far. The dolphins may have copulated but they had not conceived. It made me sad to see the difference between these dolphins and the happy, fun-loving dolphins enjoying the company of people in the performing pool. I tried to explain that they were going the wrong way about it. The situation was nothing like the sea environment and they could expect more success if they gave these dolphins love and companionship, but no one paid much attention. We were all there to consider non-verbal communication, nothing else.

I left the crowd and went unaccompanied to the opposite side of the pool. I concentrated on one of the females and I whispered to the interpreter that I would ask her to come over to me and lift her head out of the water far enough to touch me on the forehead. My head was about eight centimetres above the water. I was alone at one side of the pool, concentrating very hard and the crowd of reporters and cameramen waited at the other. There was silence. Then, within 30 seconds, the dolphin approached me. She lifted her head out of the water and very gently put her beak to my forehead.

This seemed to convince the Japanese of the possibility of this form of communication. Six hours later I was sitting in the restaurant at the railway station and I looked up at the TV screen and there I was with the dolphins. I was told that the commentary told about the psychic man from New Zealand.

I found Japanese railway stations an endless source of interest. Between 6 a.m. and 7.30 a.m. The trains are crowded. One is trapped in the middle of a human mass like tightly-packed sardines and when the doors open one has to move with that mass. The trains accelerate so fast and stop so suddenly that the whole human mass sways as one. Everyone else had their eyes tight shut as though somehow relaxing in this situation but they never seemed to miss their disembarkation point.

On the rare occasions when there was no one else in the flat I would answer the phone. In the hope that the caller spoke English I would say politely, "Good morning", or "Good afternoon".

In every case the result was the same. No reply. Clonk. They hung up on me.

I remembered that everyone else, when they answered the phone, said something that sounded like mushi-mushi so I decided to give this a go. The telephone rang. I picked it up.

"Mushi-mushi."

The result was startling. I don't know what the word means but it elicited a torrent of fast-spoken Japanese. The end result was the same but this time I was the one to hang up having not understood a word.

I didn't seem to be doing very well in communicating with people. I was glad the dolphins had been able to make contact.

Out with the
Japanese fishing fleet

It was another long and complicated journey to Iki Island, scene of the dolphin kills. We went by train to Narida airport, and flew for two hours to a port from which we took a ferry to Iki, another two-hour trip. The ferry journey, like the railway journey, was an experience not to be missed.

The ferry boat was of normal structure in every way except for the passenger accommodation which consisted of a floor with no seating facilities at all. As the crowd of travellers, up to a thousand in number, made their way onto this accommodation floor they moved along narrow walkways into partitioned areas. Each of these had space for about 10 people. The partitions were only a foot high and shoes were left outside on the walkway. Almost everyone swallowed a couple of seasick pills and made certain of the location of the aluminium vomit bowls. Then they lay down and closed their eyes. Most of them slept the journey away unless they were kept occupied by being sick.

It was the nearest thing to herding cattle I have ever seen in human transport and I laughed to myself until I nearly cried. I found that you claim your territory by sitting on the floor. When you stretch out your legs someone else is likely to use them for a pillow. Thus pinned down I watched one woman being terribly ill all the way and could do nothing to help her. She had three children with her, one of them a baby strapped on her back.

As soon as the boat berthed at Iki the whole lot of them rose up and disappeared. My shoes had been in a heap with hundreds of others but when I came to get them there were the only pair left.

From the ferry Dexter, Michi, the interpreter and I shared a taxi on the 30-minute drive to the fishing village where we were to stay. It is the home port of the fishing fleet which conducts the dolphin drives. When we arrived we found that our accommodation house was having a rush of business. An American film crew of five had arrived. Jim Nollman, an American inter-species communication expert, was sponsored by various animal welfare organisations. Greenpeace had sent an electronic sound expert. We met journalists from all over the world as well as Japanese naturalists who had taken time out from university work to help. Hardy Jones was the most conspicuous of the invaders. He was producer and director of the film crew and in a very short time he was accepted as the leader of the whole show. The film company fell victim to the need to either pay or guarantee payment for various people who were having money problems. At this remote island village, funds did not always arrive when expected and travellers cheques were not negotiable, though American dollars were acceptable. With $600 American in my pocket, and one American dollar worth 200 yen, I felt as near to being a millionaire as I will ever be.

We all settled in at the accommodation house. There was no bar but liquor could be served with meals. Fortunately we were a sober bunch and the only drinking was the enjoyment of a saki with the evening meal. This was specially prepared for us and served in one large room. Small rooms can be made into large rooms by the removal of partitions which are constructed of split bamboo and papier mache. Everyone else sat on the floor round a low table but I was given a table and chair because of my age and bulk. We were looked after by middle-aged Japanese women who did everything they could to make our stay enjoyable. We had no language in common but we had no trouble in communicating.

After the evening meal there was a couple of hours discussion in which we exchanged experiences and views.

The American recorders were going non-stop. Everything that was said was recorded. Perhaps it was just as well because the film crew generally did not know much about the business in hand. It was another filming job for them.

I saw only one cat and two dogs all the time I was in Japan. Flies and insects were very rare and, in such a busy fishing village, there were no seagulls round the wharf. Birds were apparently more or less a memory.

One morning quite early I was sitting outside the accommodation house watching the people go by. Most of the elderly people seemed to go out shopping just after daylight. They were very polite and would stop and bow. On this morning there was a stampede up the street and I followed along to see what was happening. Sixty or 70 people were gathered, talking excitedly and pointing up into the gables of a house. I strained to see what was causing so much excitement. It was seven swallows. They were the first for 15 years and had come to nest under the eaves. I was told that people made provision for birds to build nests in the hope of enticing them because, other than a few hawks, bird life is almost extinct in Japan. I fear the day may also come when Japanese will stand on the beaches yearning for the sight of a dolphin.

I was most interested to see the sophisticated underwater sound gear the Americans had brought. At home in New Zealand we had been working on the effect of various sounds on Horace, but all this electronic gear was light years away from our arrangements and what we called button-box technology, or from Bruce snorting and laughing through his snorkel or making squeaky-door sounds to test Horace. Not that it seemed to have any greater effect.

The synthesiser was a switchboard with thousands of holes. It was possible to plug in to any one of a series of these and produce a million different sounds. We tested it out. They made the sounds and I tried to relate them to dolphin or whale sounds I have heard. The idea was to find sounds to attract or repel dolphins. We might know that Bruce's chuckle or the squeaky-door noise had these effects but that is not good enough for science.

I did pick a killer whale sound that I thought ought to repel any dolphin. I have watched in the sea when a pack of killer whales, making this sound, closed in on a herd of dolphins and so mesmerised them that they were able to kill them off at will. I was to discover that the Japanese fishermen had made their own discoveries in this line and that their hammer-and-bar method, though unscientific, was deadly in the extreme.

So there we were, making plans to go off next morning. We would take all this gear and all this expertise and all these recorders and cameras and sound-makers out to wherever it was that those teeming dolphin were eating up Japan's fish harvest. The only difficulty was that none of us knew where the fishing grounds were and we did not seem to be able to hire a boat. There were 1400 fishing boats based at the port but it seemed that the skippers had held a meeting and agreed not to encourage us, so none of their boats was for hire.

Finally, after much haggling, one skipper agreed to take us. He asked $300 American a day and would take only 10 people and the gear. Arrangements were made to leave the wharf at 8 a.m. and get out amongst all these thousands of dolphins. The skipper arrived on his push-bike at 7 a.m. To say he was ready to go but he had a new condition — it was that he and his brother could do their fishing as well as carry us.

With so much gear to be transported to the wharf, Hardy procured a handcart with bicycle wheels. We loaded all the gear onto the cart and away we went. Hardy was the horse. He got in the shafts and pulled while the rest of us pushed from behind. He did most of the work until we came to a slope and then we all had to pull the cart back to stop it running over him. We developed a good coolie trot and attracted much attention. People along the street waved to us and made the dolphin sign, a swooping motion with the hand. It all seemed very friendly.

We unloaded the cart on the boat and were ready to sail at 8 a.m. I was assured that as soon as we met the dolphins the communication business would be in my hands.

52

Everyone else was at the bow waiting to get on with the great experiment — to communicate with the dolphins. Afterwards we would have the problem of communicating at a deep level with the fishermen and joining with them in the practical ways of ending the dolphin slaughter.

It was a two-hour sail to the fishing grounds. Even without a guide we could hardly have missed it. More than 1300 boats were already there, packed into a concentrated mass a couple of kilometres square providing an unbelievable sight. The noise they made was even more incredible. As we drew near they sounded like a flight of jet planes passing overhead. Every boat was rigged up with a radio and loudspeaker systems and everyone was going flat out. The noise of them all talking to one another was more than I could bear. It was clear that we would see very little of dolphin in this crowded place and in all this din, but it was also clear that our skipper had come to fish with the rest of them and that this was where we were going to stay.

We pulled into a space on the edge of the mass of boats. The skipper cut the motor. He put out no anchor, just left the boat to drift. The whole boat mass was drifting as one. He threw over two weighted handlines with lures on the ends. When these reached about 45 metres they were retrieved hand over hand as quickly as possible in the hope that the buri — yellowtail — would grab the line as it came up and thus be hooked.

The whole fleet was busy in this way and for a time the tempo of the fishing was moderate. Then someone caught a buri. The entire fleet converged on his position and went to work flat out with their lines. After a short time the boats drifted out of that school of fish and then they separated and moved about a little, scouting for more fish. As soon as one caught a fish everyone converged on him.

At certain periods of the tide when they knew the buri would not be biting, they lowered handlines to fish for squid. Our skipper and his brother caught one and they were very pleased. They knew they were assured of a good day's pay — on top of their American dollar bonanza — so they had time to be good hosts by baiting the line and inviting us to have a try.

One by one our party tried their hands but had no luck. I was the last to try and as soon as I started to pull in the line they realised that I had been at this game before and was no new hand at it like the others. It doesn't take a commercial fisherman long to recognise another. They were all smiles and rapid talk and this increased when I hooked a buri and landed it. I caught three or four before I handed back the line.

When that buri bite was over the brothers transferred their attention to the squid lines again. The members of our party were beginning to ask when we were going in search of dolphin. Perhaps I was enjoying the trip more than they were as it was a more familiar situation to me. Perhaps this is why I was lucky while they were not. I caught two squid at once and the skipper, with clear gestures, asked me if I wanted a job.

He was very gracious and very friendly, as was his brother, until I drew their attention to a spear lashed to the mast-head and asked them what it was used for. They took it down, made the dolphin sign and gave me a very clear demonstration of what they did to any dolphin that came near the boat. They stabbed the water with the spear and their eyes took on a mad frenzied look I came to recognise. It glazed their eyes whenever dolphin were mentioned; this was true of every fisherman with whom we tried to discuss dolphins. They looked as though they were under the influence of drugs or some mad kind of spell. It was becoming all too clear that there was a great barrier to communication and understanding here.

Unfortunately, the camera crew were all busy watching out for dolphins when this significant episode took place and it was not recorded on film. Through the interpreter I expressed my horror at this attitude and one of the brothers spoke back through the interpreter. He was quite polite and said he liked dolphins also but the sea-pigs were depriving fishermen of their livelihood. His words, however polite, did not convince me, not after I had seen the look in his eyes as he handled the spear.

At about 3 or 4 o'clock the boats began to head for home and we turned for port with them. It was arranged that we would go out again the next day — for the same price in dollars — and this time we would surely meet up with the dolphins. Hardy was more insistent next day and we really did leave the fishing fleet after the first bite of buri. We cruised about all day but not a sign of dolphin was seen.

The next day we crossed over from Iki Island to a small island reserve we called Massacre Island. The dolphin herd is driven many miles to be trapped and enclosed in a bay of this island, where the slaughter takes place. It is on this island that the monument to the slaughtered dolphins has been erected and this was what we had come to see.

Massacre Island is a most beautiful place, a fitting public reserve. We had a great deal of trouble getting there as no boat was for hire. Finally we found an old skipper who was not connected with the Fishermen's Union. His boat was old too and was held together with rope and hope. He gave in to the sight of the almighty dollar and agreed to take us.

We pulled in beside the wharf and began to walk round the island tracks. We reached the monument and the camera gear was brought up and I was interviewed with the monument as background. I hope the cameras got the astonished look on my face as the interpreter read the inscription. I could not believe it.

It is a beautiful piece of work seven metres high in natural black rock. The inscription in gold letters, roughly translated, reads: "In memory of the sea-pigs — may their souls rest in peace." This had been erected by the fishermen who carry out the slaughter. I sought some clarification of the puzzle from the interpreter, who explained that to the Japanese everything has a soul, even the fish they catch, but that people come first in the struggle for survival.

In the interview I was asked my views on the dolphin kill and I made it clear that I regarded it as murder. The film crew moved round the island. There had been a recent kill and some dead dolphins lay on the beaches.

Some had died there. Some had been stabbed. Some had rope marks on their tails.

The interpreter explained that the dolphin had to die because they ate the buri, the main catch. I turned over a dead dolphin and demonstrated that this was not possible, the buri was too big. They bite it in two and swallow it then, was the next claim. I was able to show the gullet of the dead dolphin and it was plain that it could not swallow buri; the gullet was much too small. The crew shot a good deal of film on this exchange.

We returned to the boat and the skipper was prevailed upon to take us to see the set nets in the bay of death. This was a terrible and daunting sight. The nets resemble cattle yards under water. The dolphins are driven into the bay and penned up in these holding yards. Some are kept there for days while the slaughter goes on, swimming in the blood of their relatives and hearing their cries as they die.

Who knows what Dexter Cate was thinking about the dolphin pens? The following year his visit was much more stealthy and dramatic but he could congratulate himself that a couple of hundred dolphin escaped because of it and perhaps many more will be saved because of the publicity his action promoted.

I did not witness a dolphin drive and I am very glad about that. I still have memories of killing the 59 Sperm whales stranded on the beach at Gisborne. I knew they had to be killed since there was no hope of saving them, and I also knew that I could do it more humanely with a lance than could be done with a rifle. Even so, for weeks afterwards I woke up with a start from terrible dreams of lashing tails and chomping jaws and pleading eyes. I would not like to go through that again as a result of watching dolphin being slaughtered.

The dolphin killing season in Japan is a three-month period between New Year and the end of March, when the family groups of dolphins amalgamate into large migration herds and move from one feeding ground to another. It is when the migratory herds are passing through or near favoured fishing grounds that the

Dolphins slaughtered by Kawana fishermen in Japan, being prepared for the processing plant. AP

The author communicating with a Japanese dolphin, showing that mental communication transcends the language barrier.

The author (back to camera) silently communicating with aborigines at Monkey Mia. The film sound man is checking for presence of sound during the silent exchange.

Golden Dolphin film crew with the author at Monkey Mia.

Volunteers wetting down one of two large-beaked whales stranded in Coromandel Harbour. The whales were later towed out through the harbour entrance, but were drowned in the process.

The large-beaked whales, mother and calf, lie side by side.

These large-beaked whales stranded on the beach at Mahia on Christmas Eve, 1984, and were lost through lack of knowledge and expertise. This was one of the very rare occasions when stranded whales have remained upright in their natural swimming position.

How it should be done. The mother-baby touch, which conveys so much to stranded dolphins and whales, ensures stress is minimised. Nelson Evening Mail

Disregarding wet and cold conditions, rescuers work to refloat one of the 80 pilot whales stranded at Tokerau Beach, Northland, in 1983.

The author on beach patrol with Bruce's Landrover in the background.

The scene that greeted Denis Richardson on the shores of Delaware Bay one morning in March 1982: seven of the group of 21 bottlenose dolphins.

Residents, MAF staff and Project Jonah members joined forces in the Great Barrier pilot-whale rescue.
NZ Herald

Aerial view of some of the 500 pilot whales stranded at Great Barrier, 1985.
NZ Herald

Helicopter to the rescue at Delaware Bay. One dolphin about to make the short flight to open water while rescuers gently right another.

fishermen go into action. Every boat is rigged for anti-dolphin action and every skipper has been coached in the part his boat will play in the operation. Each boat is rigged with a heavy piece of reinforcing steel.

It is long enough to hang right down into the water and is lashed steady with rope. A deck-hand stands by ready to strike this steel with a steel hammer.

When a herd of dolphins is sighted by a crew member three of the bright lights strung from mast-head to mast-head, and used to attract squid during night fishing, are switched on. This is the signal for everyone to stand ready. They know that a decision will soon be taken by the twelve skippers of the dolphin committee. The skippers conduct a discussion over the loudhailers to decide if there are enough dolphin to warrant breaking off fishing operations for a dolphin drive. If they decide the numbers do not warrant a drive then everyone gets on with their fishing.

Should a drive be decided upon, every boat goes into immediate action on a pre-arranged plan. There are seldom less than 600 boats out with the fleet and these quickly and quietly surround the herd. When the encirclement has been achieved, the boats are almost stern to stern. A signal is given and every boat begins a relentless banging of steel upon steel; sophisticated electronic gear could not produce a sound so terrible. The vibrations in the water play havoc with the dolphins' auditory system and the dolphins come to the surface to escape the clamour underwater. They mill about frantically and whichever way they try to swim they find they are swimming closer to the source of this terrible sound.

The leading skipper then gives the signal for the boats on the perimeter in the direction in which they want to drive the dolphins to stop banging. The sudden silence from that direction is a relief to the herd and they swim towards it and away from the vibrations which continue from every other quarter. The entire fleet moves with the herd and thus the vibrations continue in the wake and on both flanks. It is all that is needed to herd the dolphins shorewards and the speed of the drive is determined by the speed at which the dolphins try to escape the amplified underwater sounds.

When the lead boats of the drive approach the entrance to the harbour, they separate and, while still holding the wings of the boat formation so that no dolphins can escape, they give the dolphins no option but to proceed through the heads. The noise-producing rearguard and flanking boats ensure that they will not try to turn back and make a bid for freedom.

Once inside the inner harbour, with the boats blocking their rear, there is little trouble in herding them into the beautiful, tranquil bay on Massacre Island where they are enclosed in a long net. This net is kept at the ready on a boat tied to the wharf and stacked so that one man can drop the 800-metre length of it. He drops one end, backs the boat, lets the net go and can set it easily by himself. Once the small bay is closed by this 15-metre-deep nylon net, the dolphins are doomed — except on the occasion when Dexter Cate breached this net and let the dolphins go.

The slaughter begins with those dolphins not trapped in the nylon nets which form underwater holding pens. They are encircled with drag nets and pulled into the shallows. The fishermen go in with knives, spears and clubs to attack the helpless dolphin. A grinding machine on the beach reduces their bodies to pulp for fertiliser and pig food.

Thousands of dolphins die in this way every year. It is not necessary to dwell on the horrible details. Imagination can fill them in.

There are some signs now that the slaughter is to be permanently halted. We can only hope that it is not too late and that the dolphins will not become like the birds of Japan, just a memory. Whale herds were wiped out in the waters off my own country by whalers of many nations and a realisation of the tragedy taking place did not come until too late.

Other countries such as the Soviet Union and the United States appreciate that they have in the dolphins promising subjects through which to conduct investigations into alternative methods of communication. Accordingly, they have given full protection to the dolphin. New Zealand has finally followed their example after years of lobbying from a few of us.

The dolphin is the fisherman's best friend as long as they both respect their common environment, the sea. As we go on destroying the land and its fruitfulness the sea holds the key to our survival and the dolphin can teach us how to use it.

If the astute Japanese people can be helped to understand this simple fact, if they can be brought to face the abhorrence with which the rest of the world views the dolphin slaughter, if they can accept the need to experiment with protein sources other than fish to replace the fish stocks they have already depleted, there is some hope that common sense will prevail and the ocean's creatures will be protected for the use of all.

In search of
Japanese dolphins

By this time we were getting restive about the absence of
the dolphin we had come so far to see. Our skipper had an
answer.

"Night time is the best time. Hundreds of dolphin at
night".

"How much this time?"

"Still the same. $300 American."

So we piled aboard and away we went. We met a squid
boat coming in and, at our urging, the skipper asked him
over the loudspeaker if he had seen any dolphins. The two
conversed deafeningly through the microphones and then
our skipper said, "He's coming in because there are so
many dolphins he can't catch any fish."

We began to feel more hopeful. We got out to the fleet.
Approaching it was like seeing a city of lights sitting on
the water and the noise of those 1400 motors and 1400
loudspeakers coming out of the wall of boats was
shattering.

Each boat has about 20 800-watt lights. As soon as we
got there our lights went on and we started to fish,
dolphins forgotten. There were two automatic squid
catchers with multiple lures. These were let down to a
certain depth and then a winch started to wind them up.
The squid, it is hoped, will grab at the lures on the way up.
If they do they are hooked and automatically thrown off
on to the deck as the squid catcher winds down again.

Automation may be all very well but there is still a
long-handled net like a butterfly net at the ready with
which every fish that is caught by the lights is scooped up.
Five little fish swam into view and were caught. On our
return the skipper walked off at the wharf carrying them

60

in a plastic bag. I could not believe he was bothering to land them.

"Going fishing tomorrow?" I asked. "Is that bait?" But it was not. It was the catch and the catch is no joking matter.

A normal catch when a 15-metre boat with a two-man crew comes in is about 8 buri and 12 squid. This is not as meagre as it sounds. The fisherman gets paid $12 for a buri which will later sell in Tokyo for $25. For a squid he gets paid $5 and it will re-sell at $10.00

The fish are packed on the boat into different size boxes — a layer of fish, a layer of ice, cellophane, another layer of fish (still quivering) then more ice. The box is closed and roped. It has to be got from the wharf to the fishing shed which may be a mile away. In many cases Mama-san, a skipper's wife, is waiting on the wharf with a cut-down pram, hood removed and a platform built on the pram. The box is passed to her at once and she takes off with it for the fishing shed.

I felt the catch had not been worth going out for and we still hadn't seen one dolphin. We came in and went to bed feeling disappointed. Next day Hardy tried to hire a spotter helicopter but that was too expensive so he decided to film on the wharf. I was to be interviewed on the situation walking along the wharves.

This time the skindiver of the film crew had to be the horse and pull the cart while Hardy sat on top of it and directed. I walked along with the interviewer discussing fishing methods and the fish shortage. The sound man walked alongside with a microphone. The camera was on the cart being pulled along in front of us.

The public was very interested in this odd procession and there were many stoppages and unforeseen incidents. The wind was getting up; the producer was irritable at the delays. We proceeded past the skipper's house and he rushed out to invite me in. He was waved aside and we carried on. As we got further and further away from his house he followed and became more insistent. He said he had a meal prepared and I must come in and eat it. The producer abused him for interrupting the filming. I took the fisherman's side, which the producer didn't appreciate. There was almost a war on the wharf. The fisherman then invited us all to the meal. Grumbling, the film crew gave up the struggle and accepted the invitation. They were to be very glad they did.

To begin with, they were so charmed with the interior of the house that they filmed it all. Their film *Island on the Edge* had a good run in America and I was invited to go over and see it but could not afford to do so.

This unexpected visit to a Japanese home was much appreciated. The table was set with bottles of saki and dishes of delicious looking food. The uncooked buri was cut into fillets and thin slices. It looked transparent and appetising and was eaten with a dark-coloured hot sauce. It was most enjoyable. There were pauas, only a quarter the size of ours in New Zealand. They were baked in the oven in the shell, ungutted, but were delicious just the same. The skipper presented me with a bowl of sea-egg roe. He said this was especially for me. I was curious as to the value of the small bowl of this delicacy. He staggered me by saying $52 American. I later discovered that it had taken 200 sea eggs to make this one bowl of roe. It put his payment for the day out on his boat more into perspective.

After that the weather deteriorated and we were only able to go out on the boats for short periods. A fair amount of film was shot talking to people on the wharves. Finally we had an interview at the Fishermen's Union shed with the president of the union.

He made his position clear by first showing us heaps of letters from people all over the world. They were letters of protest about the dolphin slaughter which had been sent to the Japanese Government and its embassies. The Government had just packed them all up and sent them to the union. The president indicated that he wished people would mind their own business and he pointed out that we kill cattle and sheep for food. We replied that we kill humanely and not to extinction of the species.

I was anxious to get on to some more practical and useful exchanges so I asked him about depths and area of fishing grounds and the run of the currents. I wanted to find out if the dolphins were resident or migratory. If the latter, it should be possible to turn them into another migration route away from the fishing grounds. These questions really mattered. They held the key to a solution and any fisherman should be able to answer these questions about the waters in which he works.

The president became more co-operative as he tried to answer and it seemed they were beginning to believe that we had come to help and not to hinder, that we appreciated their difficulties and were anxious to work with them to find a way round them. They drew maps and diagrams and really tried to explain their situation. They also lent us a film about the surrounding and herding of the dolphins to their place of death. The actual killing had been cut out of the film but what we did see was horrible.

I asked why they didn't try to herd the dolphins away from the fishing grounds. Impossible, they said. I pointed out that as they were able to drive them 25 nautical miles shorewards against the migratory pattern, they could surely drive them off the fishing grounds and send them on their chosen path.

There was a lot of head-scratching and thinking about that. Then a bright young fisherman came up with an answer.

"But if we did that there would be twice as many of them next year." I seized on this.

"So you do admit you could drive them away if you wanted to but you just don't want to!"

They said they had tried shooting and spearing the dolphins out in the sea but had found the dolphin drive and its wholesale slaughter was the best way.

Did they care about the bad opinion of the rest of the world, I asked.

Yes, they did, they said. They had put so much pressure on the Government about the diminishing fish catch that the Government had subsidised the dolphin kill at $8 bounty per head. They insisted that this was not an incentive to kill as it took three days to herd and kill the dolphins and dispose of them in the grinder and they lost their fishing income while this was going on. Also, they said, the dolphin nets were costly, the net across the killing bay being 800 metres long and 15 metres deep.

We could see that we were achieving little apart from making world opinion clear. I left, confident that there is more than just economics involved in the desire to kill dolphins. This other feeling surfaced at a meeting of fishermen held at our hotel. The fishermen, having fortified themselves liberally with saki, began to talk about dolphin hunting and the interfering people who were staying in this very hotel.

The management of the hotel advised us to keep out of the way and the women in our party were particularly advised to lock themselves in their rooms and stay there.

Dexter Cate decided to go to the meeting uninvited. He invited the rest of us to come with him but we were not as game as he was. I had seen the glazed look come into the eyes of the fishermen just talking about killing dolphins and I decided discretion was the better part of valour.

So Dexter, game as Ned Kelly, went alone and talked and argued about dolphins all night. From the noise that came from the conference room it was a great meeting.

The weather did not improve much. It was time for me to be leaving but they kept me there until the last moment in the hope that the weather would improve and we would get out just once amongst these elusive dolphins. I stayed until the day I was booked to leave Japan.

It was a bus ride of an hour and a half to the ferry. When I stepped off the bus I was tapped on the shoulder by a young girl of about 15.

"Mr Robson?" she asked in English.

"Yes."

"Would you like me to escort you to the ferry?"

"Yes, please."

"Walk or taxi?"

"Walk."

So we walked. It turned out that she was the daughter of our skipper and he had telephoned ahead to ask her to meet me. She took me to the ferry wharf, bought the tickets, filled in the forms, got me into the right queue and then was gone. And I headed for home.

Can dolphins help us to understand one another?

Our group of media people and conservationists were gathered together in Japan for a common purpose but we differed in many respects. We came from diverse backgrounds with a wide diversity of experience between us and we went about achieving our end in different ways.

Hardy Jones and his crew were professional film-makers but although this was just another job for them they did sincerely care about the dolphins and wanted to convey a message about them to the rest of the world. The film they made, *Island on the Edge*, was shown in many countries and, as recent events seem to indicate, has had a useful impact. Even in the short term they were responsible for saving some dolphins. They paid a surprise visit to the slaughter pens and dolphins were hastily released from the pens so that they should not be photographed and create a bad impression.

Dexter Cate and the other environmentalists took another approach, being on fire for the cause. They are the colourful adventurers of our day who fly the banners and make the romantic gestures which appeal so much to the general public. They win valuable publicity and they rally public opinion. They are prepared to sacrifice themselves and pay a high price as Dexter was to prove in the following year. He went to Iki armed with telling arguments and persuasive speeches and, just in case these failed, he took along a sharp pair of net cutters as well.

After he had seen a thousand dolphins killed he could stand it no longer, so he paddled out in a kayak to the dolphin net stockyards and untied the knots in the net. As

65

the dolphins began to escape he walked them round in the water, supporting them in the upright position until they could regain their balance and swim away to safety. One large male refused to accept his help and leave because another, a female, was still trapped in the net. The three months Dexter spent in prison for the action paid off in worldwide publicity. The prison was bombarded with letters and telegrams and the people of Japan had to face the hard fact of what the rest of the world thought of them and their dolphin slaughter. It may have led their young people to think hard about the sea-pigs and wonder why they hate them so much when they also seem to love them. Could it be that, in a fearful awareness that the old ways of living are being taken from them, they are seeking a victim, a sacrifice? And what better sacrifice than the most beautiful creature in the sea?

While the film people and the sound engineers and the swashbucklers approached the problem in their various ways, I approached it in mine, the pursuit of channels of communication. I wanted to understand these Japanese fishermen and to get over to them a genuine concern and a sincere wish to see their problem and join them in an effort to find a solution. My advantage was that I, too, am a man of the sea and could feel with them. I have trained myself to think dolphin and it comes naturally to me to think fisherman. I wanted to walk for a time in the shoes of these other men, to try to suggest some practical reasons for ending the slaughter.

What possible solutions could there be?

A basic legal question was whether or not it was lawful to slaughter dolphins on the beaches of a public reserve. That idea made no progress at all and it was made clear that the Japanese did not think we had the right to pass comment on a matter of law in their country. Similarly, they have the final say about fishing regulations in their waters.

The fisherman sees the dolphin as his enemy, and, in punishing the dolphin, he seems, in some strange way, to be punishing himself for his determination to catch the last fish in the sea. He is not prepared to face the fact that it is humans, not dolphins, who are raping the sea, that the problem is not one of too many dolphins but too many fisherman.

The Japanese Government was prepared to subsidise the dolphin slaughter and pay a bounty of $8 American on each one killed. They would have been better putting their money and their legislative power into controlling the fishing situation and not allowing it to run out of control, or in reducing the pollution which is poisoning their waters. They could also have turned their attention to the situation further out to sea where the big boats of the multi-national interests are depleting the world's resources and destroying the balance of the environment.

If the present trend of diminishing catches continues there will be no fish left in Japanese waters within a few years and it will not be the fault of the dolphins. At one time the excuse for the killing was that the Japanese needed the dolphins for food just as we need sheep. My reply to that is that we do not try to wipe out the sheep. We husband them and eat the increase and when we kill, we kill humanely.

Dolphins are no longer considered edible as recent tests have found high levels of mercury and pesticide in them. So a huge grinding machine is used to chew up dolphin carcasses for conversion into fertiliser or pig food. The same pollution is present in the tissue of the fish being caught for human consumption. And the contaminated fertiliser and stock food produced from the dolphin carcasses puts the pollution back onto the land and into the stock which will supply people's food. But governments may choose to ignore such realities.

The vast fishing fleet I went out with has only a few years left to it and most of the fishermen made it clear that they do not intend their sons to be fishermen. In reply to my questions they made it clear in sign language that they wanted their sons to go into clerical jobs. In fact, most of them seemed to be aiming their sons at the Post Office rather than at the family fishing boat.

It seems, then, that hard economic reality will change the Japanese fisherman's world. Much though they love their fish, the Japanese will have to settle for other sources of protein. It would be of advantage to New Zealand if interesting books on alternative eating patterns were translated into Japanese, and if there were more direct promotion of what this country has to offer instead of the unesteemed lamb. This might lead to a new market among all those young people who, if their fathers have their way, will be over-fishing the Post Office.

Apart from these economic factors, I felt there was something much deeper and darker in the drive to kill dolphins. I saw it in the eyes of the fishermen at Iki Island and I saw it again in the eyes of the Japanese who attended the International Whaling Conference in Washington in 1980. At the conference they were emphatic that Japan would not stop killing whales or dolphins, which, they declared, were nothing but pirates exploiting the sea. They were not concerned in the least about the possibility of wiping out a species.

I found great difficulty in reconciling this attitude with the fact that at Iki people seem to think about dolphins all the time, their lives are haunted by dolphins. Children wear dolphin badges and have dolphin insignia on their schoolbags. People make the dolphin sign, a swooping with the hand, and everyone knows it. They seem to feel very strongly the natural attraction of humans towards dolphins and yet have adopted a chilling and barbaric hatred to disown that feeling.

The total absence of dolphins when we searched so thoroughly for them convinced me that the herds under attack were not residents of the fishing grounds and competitors for the fish in them. They were migrating herds going past 20 or more nautical miles out from the coast. Since it is so easy to drive them all those miles to the beach, they could just as easily be driven seawards and hurried on their migratory way for the fishermen knew that their steel bars and hammers were a deadly and frightening tool with which to herd dolphins.

No, I was sure that they wanted to kill; they enjoyed it. So I was overjoyed to hear that the killing of the dolphins seems now to have been halted. Perhaps the film made under such difficulties and the publicity won so hard by Greenpeace and Dexter Cate made some impression. Certainly the Japanese are most sensitive to criticism and for the world at large to see them as barbarians would cut them deeply. It was reported in 1984 that a stranded herd of pilot whales had been rescued after two days' hard work by Japanese. This seems to indicate a great change of attitude.

I was prepared to admit that Japanese fishermen had a problem but it did not seem to be a real problem of poverty. The homes looked comfortable and the children seemed well cared for. Even in this remote fishing village, they were playing with expensive toys such as battery-powered robots. The meal we enjoyed so much was not what one would expect in the home of a fisherman and it must have been costly.

Their problem is one of a traditional staple diet dying out because they have mismanaged their resource. They have fished out their waters and they are rapidly killing off by pollution what still lives there.

We must not allow them to come and do the same in our waters and we must take care not to do it ourselves. The oceans are the property of all people and we will have to answer to future generations for our stewardship of our coastal waters.

For 40 years we have been compelled by law to conserve New Zealand coastal waters but our governments do not seem to understand or be too concerned about the possible long-term effects of big fishing ventures. They look only to the short-term profit to be gained from opening our waters to international fishing interests. They should go to Japan and take a look at the consequences of such thinking while there is still time. A New Zealand fisherman can go to Japan and argue with a small-boat owner and tell him that what he is doing is not only wrong but stupid. Who can argue with the big fishing interests? They are faceless and want to hear only one word — profit.

If we wonder how the astute Japanese came to their present dilemma concerning food and resource survival, we should look again at where New Zealand is being led and question whether our resources are still in our own hands. If we care about the sea as our lifeline and if we care about dolphins, we should look to what is happening here before we expound on the sins of the Japanese. Dolphins are being killed in our waters as they were at Iki; they even die occasionally in the tuna nets of the joint-venture super-seiners. Of course, we have enlightened legislation and provision has been made for the dolphins to be allowed to escape from the nets, but if a skipper does not choose to delay the operation and back off to release the dolphins they will die in the net.

Who is out on the sea to police the action? If the skipper has to answer in big money to big business is it likely that he will worry about saving dolphins? And will the men in the boardroom counting the profits care at all? Dolphins are dying along with the tuna, and cold indifference and love of profit can be just as deadly as the killing frenzy so we need not pour all the guilt upon the Japanese.

The need to communicate has never been more urgent. Words are so often a barrier because people make them mean different things. Language divides us. I felt close to the Japanese fishermen when we exchanged thoughts about our common experiences but I felt light years away from them when their eyes took on that glazed look of hatred with the mention of dolphins or when I stood before that incomprehensible monument erected to the dolphins by their murderers on Massacre Island.

If we are to share the oceans we have to learn to understand one another. If we can communicate with dolphins perhaps they can teach us to communicate with one another. The dolphin evokes so much love and yet so much hate that it must be a truly powerful force, and one we could learn to use.

Dolphins in
Aboriginal dreamtime

There is at the present time considerable activity amongst film-makers on the dolphin trail. They move about the world from place to place wherever dolphin encounters are reported, but not too often would they find material for their film from such a place as the dry lands of Australia.

I became involved with Golden Dolphin Films after a whale stranding in which all the whales were lost on the coast of New South Wales. A group of freelance Australian film-makers were so moved by this event that they set about raising finance to make a film which would educate the Australian public on the ways by which they could avert another such tragedy. They had heard that in New Zealand new rescue methods were being promoted and implemented with some success. When they rang me from Australia I promised to help them in every possible way. I supplied them with information and I invited them to come and stay with the Robsons while filming in New Zealand.

The director of Golden Dolphin Films was Bob Loader and its producer was Tristram Miall. The film they made was titled *Stranded*. It was a great success and was shown worldwide on the TV series *Our World*. Bruce and I figured in the New Zealand sequences of the film. We were pictured at home getting ready to go out patrolling the beach — collecting our gear, loading up the Rover and driving off down the road. We had to do this scene about eight times as interested parties kept appearing on the pavement and spoiling the shot.

The main filming was done at Mahia beach and we spent a long day from 5 a.m. To 11 p.m. making it. First we needed a whale, and I conjectured where we might be likely to find a carcass. By searching the beach from a helicopter we found one where I had suggested. We dug it up and Bruce and I were filmed measuring it and removing some of the teeth. Bruce was then sent off to drive up the long, empty beach in the Land-Rover as though patrolling while the helicopter with camera crew aboard flew low over him. Next I was filmed talking about strandings, their causes and what should be done.

It was blowing hard but the helicopter later made a few runs over the sea and some dolphins were sighted and filmed. Finally, we all settled down to wait for the sunset and the cameramen were rewarded for their patience by the most spectacularly beautiful sunset anyone could hope to film.

While the film-makers were in Hawke Bay they became interested in the stories everyone had to tell about Horace who'd left us at the end of the previous summer. They looked through my collection of slides and photographs and got enthusiastic about investigating the possibilities of inter-species communication.

They began to process the *Stranded* film, but before they got far with it, they had news that the wild dolphins had returned to Monkey Mia, a beach caravan park in Western Australia regularly visited by dolphins. This was their chance. Temporarily shelving the processing job in favour of an attempt to film non-verbal communication in action they returned to Australia post-haste. Later they telephoned me from Sydney and asked me to join them. I told them that I could do so but that my time was limited as I was scheduled to talk on whale strandings in Sydney and Melbourne in three weeks' time.

"Meet us in Sydney the day after tomorrow," was the reply. "We'll pay your fare from this end."

The Australians were hopeful of recording something significant in the way of mental communication. None of us were to know how unexpectedly they would succeed: that the communication would not be between dolphin and human but between human and human without any language link.

Once again we were to discover that trying to learn

from dolphins can lead us into a better understanding of one another.

Two days later I was on my way to Sydney to meet the film team and proceed with them to Perth, then by small plane to Denham and finally, by Land-Rover to Monkey Mia.

At least, that had been the plan. But half way across the Tasman, we learned that the Australian internal airline was on strike. When I reached Sydney I was met by Bob's secretary who informed me that the crew had chartered a small plane and, in order to get to the location on schedule, had departed two hours previously with a full load. I was to get myself to Monkey Mia by any possible means and as quickly as I could.

It took two days of sitting about twiddling my thumbs to get to Perth and when I did at last get there the strike was still on. There was no bus or train service to Monkey Mia and I didn't feel like walking the remaining 1200 kilometres of the journey. I spent the next two days abusing airways officials until I was finally offered a seat in a small plane. A booking clerk at last realised where I was heading.

"Hell, mate, you want to go to Shark Bay and the only way to get there is on the milk-run plane."

It was due to depart at 7 a.m. The next morning on its regular trip to service the outback airstrips. I had little luggage to worry about. I'd parted company with that and had been told it would follow me sometime. I got out to the airport by 6.30 a.m. and the taxi driver who took me there enquired crossly what the hell I was doing out at this ungodly hour. I told him I was on my way to Monkey Mia and got the usual answer.

"Where the hell is that?"

I asked him if he knew where Shark Bay was and he did.

"You must be running away from the police to go to that godforsaken place," he commented. "Are you in the drug business?"

So I told him that my absence was holding up the shooting of an important film and enjoyed the look in his face. I'm not sure whether he believed it but he did wish me luck "out beyond the wilderness", as he put it.

By 7 a.m. There were five of us waiting for the milk plane but there was no sign of it.

"Sit over there and I'll give you the nod when it comes," we were told.

We sat. We waited. Then we got the nod and rose as one person to go over to the desk. We need not have hurried. The plane was fog-bound and they didn't know when it would come.

"Sit there . . . but don't go away . . . It may get here."

Don't go away? Where was there to go? Only Monkey Mia existed; it was like Mecca, somewhere ahead to be striven towards. I caused some difficulty with my booking because I wanted to go as far north as the plane ever went and they would have to leave me at an airstrip some kilometres out from Shark Bay. They asked anxiously if I was sure someone would be there to meet me when dropped. The clerk surveyed all the passengers and said I must embark last because I was the biggest and there wasn't much room on the plane.

We waited and waited. Just before 9 o'clock a young fellow in uniform trousers and a white shirt appeared and asked passengers for the milk run to follow him. We thankfully carried our small cases out to the plane — a very small plane. As instructed, I waited for the other passengers to embark while the pilot stowed our luggage in the tail section. He asked me where I was bound and when I told him he said, "You will be last off so you have to be the first on." And all the other passengers had to climb out again to let me get in up front.

"Fasten your seat belts," said the pilot but, to my disgust, mine was about 12 centimetres short of going round me. More delay. I asked if anyone happened to have a piece of strong cord on them and one passenger, probably a farmer going home, did have a piece. I tied a fisherman's secure but fast-releasing knot and trussed myself up as securely as any other passenger. I have flown before in small planes but I never saw one so small take on such a heavy load.

Then we were airborne and, judging by the position of the sun, flying north. We were only flying for half an hour when we made the first landing, and for the next six and a half hours, that was the pattern. Below us would appear a strip of clay which turned out to be as primitive an airstrip as could be imagined. At the first landing I could see a steel drum mounted on a post. The pilot hopped out, took a parcel and a carton from the luggage rack, ran to the drum, lifted the lid and put the freight inside, then back to the plane and a swift take-off, just clearing the brush as we ran out of track.

Sometimes a passenger would get off and always a car was waiting. Sometimes a car was awaiting the arrival of the plane to collect a parcel and take it away to goodness knows where as there were no houses or other buildings visible even when the plane was airborne. One strip was tar-sealed and here the tiny plane refuelled before taking off again to fly along the edge of the desert. The heat in the plane was intense and we ended up in shorts and singlets, but even that was no relief from the streaming perspiration.

Finally, there were only two of us left. The other passenger was reporting to a new job in the salt ponds we could see ahead of us. When he left the plane he had travelled 1100 kilometres in his search for employment. The salt ponds cover a large area and are a fine sight from the air. Each is a different shade of blue or green, depending on the state of the evaporation process. The water comes in from the sea and is dammed at high tide in order to retain it. Then it is left to evaporate until it has dried out to a thick crust of salt which is gathered by mechanical harvesters.

The next stop was to be my destination. I looked and looked but could see nothing that resembled an airport but we came lower and lower and finally landed on another clay strip. I must admit that it was superior to the other landing places because it had a small tin shed instead of the usual box on a pole and the shed sported a wind sock on its roof. There was also something like a dog kennel to put the freight in.

The pilot pulled up in a cloud of dust close to the dog kennel. He put out the mail and the freight and then he put out my suitcase. He asked anxiously whether anyone was expecting me and I shook my head.

"Well, I'm sorry but I can't wait. Just stay put. If no one else comes to get you, someone will come to get the mail and the freight and they'll pick you up."

We waved goodbye and he gunned the motor and took off, leaving a cloud of dust from one end of the strip to the other. I discovered that the shed was locked and the dog box was too small to get into out of the sun. I must have looked a pathetic sight, 8000 kilometres away from home, sitting on my little case hard up against the side of the shed and still not able to get out of the sun.

All this in search of dolphins . . . when I could go out in a boat at home and see them almost any day. Dolphins . . . cool and comfortable in the sea while I sat there lost in the Australian outback, slowly melting away.

The pilot must have done me the favour of buzzing the Denham Post Office as he flew over it on his way home. Within 15 minutes I saw what looked like a column of dust snaking its way skywards above the endless stunted brush. It got nearer and nearer and finally I saw a Land-Rover emerge from the scrub and come towards me. The cloud followed and, as soon as the vehicle stopped, completely obliterated it. Then Bob, the film director, swam out of the cloud.

"Where in hell have you been?" he asked crossly.

"Sitting here waiting for you," I replied.

He collected the mail and freight and we were off, stirring up the dust cloud once more on the way to Monkey Mia and journey's end.

First stop was Denham Post Office where he delivered the mail and I restored my dehydrated body with three cans of drink. Then we took off, into the dust again. There was no danger of a collision even had there been any other cars as the cloud would have given warning of any approaching vehicle. And there were no animals in danger of being run into; I had not seen an animal of any sort since I left Perth. There was no bird life, no real trees, no water or mud holes and no fences or gates to mark out land rights. There was just nothing but dust and the clay from which it came, and stunted brush.

At last we turned a bend in the road and the caravan park and the beach came into view like an oasis. I knew now why the caravanners and the dolphins come back year after year to this beautiful, tranquil place. Monkey Mia consisted of the owner's house and a store at which things could be bought amazingly cheaply. Its little main street runs parallel with the beach and has hot showers, toilets and a generating plant. The caravans are parked on either side of it and some people spend the entire winter there. Drinking water is brought in by tanker from 30 miles away.

I met the film crew and the proprietors, Wilf and Hazel, and then I was taken down to the clean, sloping sandy beach. And there they were, the dolphins. I could see the dorsal fins of five of them swimming slowly about on the surface of a sea which never gets rough. I walked to the water's edge and they slowly advanced to meet me until their heads were resting on the sandy bottom. They sent me greetings with open mouths and guttural sounds which needed no interpretation. I waded in up to my knees and we got acquainted with one another. The bizarre journey somehow seemed worth it.

We had freshly baked scones and tea in Hazel's cool living room and then a hot shower and back to the beach to the dolphins. We ended the day with a magnificent meal Hazel had prepared for the whole film crew. Before, during and after the meal all the talk was of dolphins and it ended only when the diesel generator switched off at 11 p.m. We made our way back to our caravans by torchlight. The temperature at night was 35 degrees and sleep came hard.

First thing in the morning the crew were down at the beach ready to start shooting. I was confident that I could get the attention of the dolphins and that they would do what I mentally asked them to do. A 12-year-old boy was asked to stand waist-deep in the water and I said I would concentrate on getting the dolphins to swim between his legs. I would form an image of the dolphin doing this and fully expected to see it happen even as I pictured it.

Suddenly we heard cheerful voices. Two of the campers were at the water's edge, one carrying a bucket and the other carrying a plastic bag full of fish. In a flash I lost all control of the dolphins and they lost any interest in me as they flocked around begging for their expected breakfast. Filming stopped, to the disappointment of the campers, until they went away.

"Right. We'll begin again." Bob said. But it was no use.

Campers had travelled hundreds of kilometres to feed dolphins and had caught all this fish to do it. They were not going to miss the chance of being filmed. They began to arrive in their numbers, every one carrying a bucket or a bag of fish. I'm sure they must have been saving fish for a week and as soon as the camera turned they fed it out to the greedy dolphins who had never had it so good and who certainly had no inclination to do anything else.

We did some filming with a gill net and a dinghy gathering samples of the food available for the dolphins without hand feeding. When we got back to the beach the dolphins had gone. We could only wait for them to return and, as soon as they did, back came the campers with their buckets and plastic bags. Bob called a conference to discuss the situation but it was agreed that all we could do was wait and hope for a quiet moment with the dolphins and without the bucket brigade. In the meantime they would shoot the back-up sequences.

I understood that this situation was different from that we had known with Horace. Horace had been alone and had been desperate for friendship and company. This lot needed no one. They were just out for fun and free fish and who could blame them? It proved impossible to use them for demonstration purposes as they did not want to do anything else while the fish was on offer. Everywhere the film crew went, the campers went too. If the dolphins were not performing well for the cameras the campers certainly were.

However, though we had to accept disappointment concerning our initial plans, the film crew was about to find itself filming non-verbal communication in a completely unexpected way.

A party of five Aborigines arrived on location. Bob had recently come to know about this tribe who lived way up in the Northern Territory. They were called the Dolphin People because of a sacred legend in their tribe. The film company chartered a plane and flew them to Monkey Mia from their northern home. It was found then that they could only stay one night. Just before they left a member of their tribe had died and, since they were all people of some standing in the tribe, it was essential that they should be with their people at that time. There were four headmen and their leader who was called Alex.

Every year this tribe holds two ceremonies in honour of the dolphin legend. The first ritual may be attended by all members of the tribe but the other is of a more sacred nature. It may only be witnessed by males and, even then, by men past the age of adolescence. What takes place at this ceremony is a secret closely guarded from the young people and women of the tribe. Alex is the master of ceremonies at these rituals. He is known as the Dolphin Grandmother and is the main source of knowledge about the legend. There is no written information on this matter and it is his task to see it handed on to another generation. It was quite clear to me that Alex, the Grandmother of the legend, would make his own decision about how much was to be disclosed in this TV situation, although he made it clear through the interpreter that he was prepared to give some information.

Because their stay was to be so brief, the film crew lost no time in filming the sequences for which the Aborigines had been engaged. With cameras and soundmen all around us, the Aborigines and I were directed to walk down to the water to the dolphins. The idea was to capture the reaction of the Aborigines to the meeting. They were overwhelmed. Everyone was surprised since their tribal identity is based on the dolphin. I got a mental flash from them at once and burst out with what I saw.

"They've never seen a dolphin at close range before," I said.

"How do you know that?"

"I know it. Ask the interpreter."

By this time the men were in the water with the dolphins. They patted them and stroked them and jabbered away in their own language. The director asked the interpreter to ask them if they had ever been so close to a dolphin before. Their reply was clear: they had not.

They stood in the water and waved their arms to the horizon. I knew that they were saying they had only seen them way out on the sea. I was beginning to realise with great excitement that this ancient people might have retained intact the ability for non-verbal communication.

Alex's big scene was the one in which he would explain the background of the dolphin legend. He was positioned facing me with a background of his companions behind him. The cameras whirred as Alex spoke to me. His combination of fast speech and quick hand gestures conveyed not a thing to anyone but before he had finished speaking I had in my mind the picture he was trying to convey.

Bob, the director, gave his impression of what Alex had said. I disagreed with him and he asked for my version. With the picture I had received from Alex still in my mind, I related what I took from it. I saw the expression on Alex's face that he was receiving back the picture he had given.

Bob turned to the interpreter for confirmation and was told that I had more or less repeated what Alex had said. The mental image I received from Alex told this story:

Long ago, in the area where his ancestor lived, there was a large island but it had no springs of fresh water and was therefore uninhabitable. One day a large shark pursued a dolphin into the inshore waters of this island and finally bit it in two. So great was the speed of the chase that the front part of the dolphin, which was out of the water and in the air in its attempt to evade the snapping jaws, flew on through the air and landed with terrific force on the island. A large crater was caused by the impact and this began to fill with water from an underground spring. The island was then habitable and has been the home of the tribe since that day.

Someone asked what happened to the tail end of the dolphin. Did the shark eat it? There was some animated talk and it was clear that the answer was no. I was able to tell them what Alex was saying as I got the picture plainly in my mind as he spoke. The distinctive shape of the tail-end of the dolphin, flukes and all, can still be seen in the face of the sea-cliff on the island. From this time on, I felt I was accepted by the men as one of themselves — to a certain degree.

How the legend is commemorated in the secret rituals is anyone's guess and that is the way Alex and his mates intend it to remain. But one may guess that the legend demonstrates that the forefathers of the tribe knew the concern and attraction dolphins seem to have for humans.

At the end of the day, the company gathered round a fire on the beach. Alex insisted on sitting beside me. When this sequence was being filmed it was rather hoped that in the friendly and relaxed atmosphere a little more information about the tribal rituals might be forthcoming. After some companionable discussion, Bob suggested that Alex might sing a dolphin song to close the day. I could have told him then that Alex had not the slightest intention of giving away the tribal secrets to the TV camera.

Alex, of course, refused. Then everyone tried to persuade him, enlisting the interpreters in the effort. There was much rapid discussion and then Alex agreed — on condition, the interpreter said, that everyone joined in by clapping hands or marking time. This was so successful that Alex was called on for two more songs. Then Bob thanked him for his dolphin songs. The fire was doused. It was time for bed.

I walked back to the caravan site with the interpreter. I told him that I didn't believe Alex had been singing a dolphin song and that each verse was a repetition of the last.

"You're right on both counts," he said.

Alex had been making up a song as he went along. It was just a polite thank you to the film crew for bringing them to see the dolphins and giving them a journey by air. It was a suitable and proper song for the occasion, but it certainly was not a dolphin song. The ritual song is a secret, the interpreter said, and nothing would make Alex divulge it to the world and the TV camera.

One wonders how these first Australians have managed to retain the ability to communicate through mental images and to recognise the ability in others? Do their fellow Australians of more recent times have any idea of what they could learn if they wanted to?

In the people of the Dolphin tribe, compelled to live close to nature as their ancestors did, one can get a glimpse of the vast area of knowledge and understanding into which mental image communication, free from words, could take us. The rest of us, softened by over-civilisation, have lost our basic skills and put up barriers of words — words which lay bare differences of race and culture, of educational standards and language.

The people doing much to break down barriers and open up understanding are those who believe we have something to learn from communication with the dolphins. They are not people in universities and research laboratories but those, like the Golden Dolphin film team, who get together what money they can and go where things are really happening — out to the beaches and the bays and even into the dry heart of Australia to find a man like Alex, the Dolphin Grandmother and keeper of the legend. True seekers don't search for knowledge in office or library; they go out to find it and they take it where it comes.

Regrettably, my engagements to lecture in Sydney and Melbourne prevented me from accepting the invitation of the film company to go with them to their next location up in the Northern Territory, home of Alex and his Dolphin People. It was hoped in this sequence to capture on film evidence of the dolphin legend. I heard later that they were given a great welcome but, as I bade them all farewell, I knew very well that they would obtain little proof and that the real story of the sacred rituals would be jealously guarded by the Dolphin People.

I was sorry to say goodbye to the dolphins, even though they had not been good subjects for the film. In spite of them, the film *The Dolphin Touch* was successfully completed and is probably still showing in various parts of the world, still educating the public on the need to care for the sea creatures for our own sake.

Wilf and Hazel Wilson have established a dolphin welfare group to help them see that no harm will befall their charges in what must be the most remote but the most friendly caravan site in the world.

Saving the whales

Whales and dolphins have always held a strange fascination for humanity. Evidence of this dates back to the earliest recorded myths and legends. In today's world it sometimes seems as though the survival of the human race is in jeopardy and these creatures of the sea, air-breathing mammals like ourselves, have become a symbol of the determination to survive.

We have staked our future on the power of words and logic and have perhaps allowed other intuitive faculties to weaken. We observe with wonder that these sea creatures who, millions of years ago, lived on land, have retained and refined mental abilities far in advance of man's use of his brain. So we become aware of the possibility of learning from them. And in fighting to save them from destruction — for we have excelled in advancing our destructive abilities — we feel we may in some way save our hopes for the future.

I have never accepted the idea that such creatures would wantonly and needlessly destroy themselves. Having rejected the suicide theory as a cause of strandings I set myself the task of researching every reported stranding on the coasts of New Zealand. This long, narrow country has a formidably long coastline yet many strandings occur in the same areas. This immediately suggested that geographic features are part of the stranding pattern. It soon became clear that shelving sandy beaches were the most common sites for strandings.

The first essential for my project was a network of spotters drawn from people living close to the beach in the most likely areas. With their help and the help of the telephone I was able to get to the scene of strandings during, or even before, the actual stranding. Spotters were often able to pick up what I refer to as phase one of a stranding. They would see a herd of whales swimming past on a course parallel to the beach and observe them begin to swim about in a confused manner. Then one whale would detach itself and start to swim shorewards, often followed by others.

Studies of such behaviour have shown that the best course of action to prevent a stranding is as follows: The spotter should first notify the Department of Conservation who have assumed responsibility for marine mammals. The spotter should then return to the scene and do everything possible to keep the whales off the beach. The basic ploy is to create a noise barrier between the beach and the herd. Speedboats cruising up and down between the two is one way. Otherwise, as much underwater sound as possible should be made, such as banging iron bars or hammers together, or even banging rocks together underwater — anything that produces strongly vibrating sounds. On one Northland beach a group of schoolchildren prevented a stranding by screaming at the whales. When successful, all this noise in the water forces the whales to turn seawards.

My father had stressed his belief that if you keep your eye on nature you will find the answers you seek. Slowly, by doing this, my lessons were learned. I came to recognise the climatic conditions and geographical features which can cause confusion in a herd. I saw the social patterns of the herds, their loyalty to the death. I understood the balancing technique required to float off a whale, the things necessary to protect it while it was ashore, the painless method of putting down those which could not be saved, and how to record an incident. Every stranding was a case in which the normal behavioural patterns of the group had broken down. Every situation was a learning opportunity for me.

At the time I started this work, the rest of the world seemed to know little and care less about what was happening on the beaches of New Zealand. Once records began to be kept and made available, and specimens and carcasses shipped out to overseas researchers, interested people came to realise that in New Zealand waters we have one of the finest marine laboratories in the world. It was clear that while some highpowered and well-financed research was going on there had been little opportunity for first-hand experience of strandings and few researchers had had access to reports of pre-stranding behaviour. Demand for information, photographs and specimens has since been steady.

We learned an important lesson in the catching of dolphins for Marineland. The first caught were laid on their side on the deck and after examination some of them, for any one of a number of reasons, were considered unsuitable and released. It was then observed that they couldn't swim away but lay on their sides in the water and circled round and round until they managed to regain their balance. Learning from this, we made sure that the next dolphins caught were laid on their stomachs and propped up in this position. It was found that when these dolphins were released they could swim off straight away.

We had found an answer to the pattern of stranding behaviour in which a mammal refloated after lying on its side on the beach would swim round in circles and end up back on the beach. It was not a determined suicide attempt. It was a lack of balance.

This was demonstrated in 1965 at a beach camping ground in Hawke Bay, where a stranding was averted. New Zealand is a farming country and one thing New Zealanders are good at is the care of animals. One sunny morning in January, campers at Clifton camping ground, many of them farming families on holiday, awoke to find about 50 pilot whales on the beach and the rest of the herd swimming about on the surface in an upset manner and obviously preparing to come to join their mates on the beach.

(We have learned since that as long as some of the herd remain in the sea, it is usually possible to refloat the animals on the beach. They have someone to swim out to and their family instinct will draw them seawards).

These campers were not solely concerned for the whales. They simply didn't want their holiday ruined by dead whales on the beach and they were determined to get them off and back into the sea. They remembered the procedure on the farm at home for getting a cast sheep on to its feet. A sheep cast on the ground needs to be held and steadied until it can get its balance back to walk away. These pilot whales got the same treatment. They were put into the water facing out to sea, each one held by about six people in the wash of the tide, then pushed out. They heard the calls of the herd in the water and they swam straight out to the them. All except five of them were saved.

In the same year, another mass stranding of pilot whales at Cape Campbell in the South Island was also thwarted by determined farmers. One of them saw the key animal come ashore and saw groups of others joining up and preparing to come to it on the beach. Burying dead sheep was enough for one farmer and he was determined not to have to start burying whales so he called in his neighbours to help, got his tractor and rolled the whales back into the sea as fast as they came ashore. The suicide theory doesn't stand up against a farmer who is determined that whales are not going to die on his beach. From a herd of 100, only two failed to make it back to sea.

Whangarei harbour in the northern part of the North Island is a favourite place for whale strandings because of the shape of its estuary and the false readings this gives on the whale sonar.

Two hundred and seven pilot whales stranded themselves in the harbour in 1968 and all rescue attempts failed. As darkness fell, the residents could work no longer and reluctantly left the whales to their fate. Their sadness that night, listening to the splashing and squeaking in the darkness, turned to joy the next morning when they found that the herd had somehow taken advantage of the high tide and saved itself. Among the few dead left behind were a lactating female and a young calf, probably the key animals which caused the stranding. It is possible that these may have died and that the herd then felt free to save itself when the tide came along to help them.

Whangarei harbour was the scene of another interesting stranding incident in 1978, this time a joint rescue carried out by humans and dolphins. Local residents were by this time more familiar with the stranding habits of dolphins and whales and when a herd of about 150 pilot whales tried to come ashore in the estuary, the locals successfully intercepted all but two. The herd accepted defeat in this spot but moved to a more remote beach in the harbour and came ashore there.

By the time they were discovered and rescue arrangements were under way, many of the whales were dead and those who survived and were refloated seemed reluctant to leave the scene. A jet boat moving between the shore and the survivors prevented them from beaching again but they seemed unsure which way to swim to safety, probably because they were receiving conflicting readings on their sonar due to the maze of banks and channels in the harbour.

Then a group of dolphins came to the rescue. They swam in amongst the whales and led them into a deeper channel which led to an exit from the harbour. A helicopter was hovering overhead and from there it was clear that the dolphins were leading the whales to the open sea. Some dolphins took lead positions out in front while others swam among the distressed whales. When set nets barred the way to freedom, the lead dolphins guided the herd round the end of the nets. When the deep channel leading to the harbour mouth was reached, the dolphins broke away, leaving the last part of the rescue to the jet boats which had followed the procession up the harbour and which then shepherded the whales to the exit and to freedom.

The many people who took part in this rescue were adamant that the dolphins communicated continuously with the whales and that some form of understanding and communication passed between dolphins and humans, most of whom were Fisheries Officers.

There is another reported incident in which dolphins came to the rescue of whales on the New Zealand coast. It was in September 1983 and occurred at Tokerau Beach, Doubtless Bay, Northland. A farmer's wife was getting the breakfast ready. Standing at her kitchen window, she looked down to the beach where she could see some activity. It was a cold, bleak day — too cold, she thought, for anyone to be out collecting scallops.

It turned out that what she was watching was a stranding of pilot whales. By the time the neighbours had been alerted and had gathered, there were 80 of them on the beach. Some of the people were familiar with the techniques I had been advocating; two of them had attended lectures on the subject in Auckland. They knew what to do.

The school bus passed on its rounds and the driver stopped to have a look. There was no way the children were going to miss this drama by going on to school, so people aged from five to 65 worked together in the cold and the wet. They remembered to talk kindly to the whales, to reassure them and lessen their shock. They kept them covered and wet until the rising tide brought deep water to refloat them.

When there was enough water to buoy them up, they manhandled them round to face the sea. Four young whales died from the shock and stress of the situation but 76 were returned to the sea. Their exhausted rescuers then had the rewarding experience of seeing dolphins swim in amongst the whales and guide them safely out from the beach into deep water. This rescue was featured in the BBC Wildlife Journal in 1984.

There have been many reported cases of dolphins helping a drowning person back to the beach, and even repeatedly lifting a skindiver to the beach when it seemed he was in trouble, but these are the first reported instances of dolphins coming to help other cetacea to safety.

Tokerau beach was the scene of another successful rescue in October 1985 — same place, same time of the year — when 150 pilot whales were helped safely away by local residents with the loss of only three.

The Whangarei stranding experiences taught us a great deal. In my experience I have found that a facility for non-verbal communication seems to be sharpened by a sense of urgency, by danger, or by a concern for someone else. Is it possible that the urgency of the whales' danger and the level of concern generated by those trying to help them was the trigger for the communication felt between animals and humans?

It was also learned from these strandings that the method of creating a sound barrier to keep whales away from the beach must only be practised on an open beach where the whales can safely be driven seawards. In an estuary of enclosed waters the whales are already in some confusion because deep-water channels threading between mud-flats and sand-flats have given them a series of contradictory readings on their echo-location systems. Noise will only further confuse them and drive them into more danger. The best way to help them in this situation is to use small boats to block their further progress up the estuary. Such boats should approach the herd from a landward direction even if it means they have to be carried overland. If the boats approach from the seaward side they will only drive the whales further into the estuary.

When they meet the obstruction caused by the boats the whales need to be given time to settle down and quietly assess the new situation. Once they can be persuaded to turn about — the only noise being used perhaps a gentle tapping on the sides of the boats — they can be shepherded into the deep channels and towards the harbour mouth, a watch being kept that they do not turn off into side channels.

This procedure will not work if any stranded whales are still alive but are being left behind. In that case the whales will break past the shepherding boats to try to return to their mates in trouble. In 1978 in Manukau Harbour, near Auckland, a herd of 180 whales, almost at the estuary mouth, suddenly responded to the cries of their comrades left behind and surged back past the escorting boats. All of them were lost. The first part of that rescue attempt should have been to silence all those too weak or injured to be rescued.

Mahia Beach in Hawke Bay is a well-known stranding spot and, to judge from Maori history, always has been. One theory is that since Mahia was once an island, the whales are trying to follow a race-memory of a passage through. The real explanation is certainly geographic: the peninsula is a natural whale trap. Shaped like a large fish-hook, it has a confusing effect on the echo-location system of the whales. When they swim into the hook there is a large bluff on their seaward side. They get a more favourable reading from the gently sloping beach, so they turn that way.

On one occasion I witnessed a stranding averted by the whales themselves. I was alone on the deserted Mahia beach when 19 pilot whales, each one about six metres in length, swam straight into the trap. They veered away from the seaward bluff when it gave them a bad reading and headed straight for the beach. They grounded and there was nothing I could do to help. I walked down to the edge of the water and listened to them squeaking and grunting. Occasionally one would lift a tail fluke and slap it down on the water as though in annoyance rather than panic. They waited and I waited.

As each wave deepened the water they turned a little and finally got themselves facing out to sea. As bigger waves came in they lifted into them and floated free of the bottom. When all were in the clear they waited for a really big wave and swam off into it.

It was a copybook lesson on what we should do to help them in a stranding. They had not lain on their sides and therefore hadn't lost their balance. They had understood that they must face out to sea if they were to be able to take advantage of a big wave and not let it wash them further inshore. They kept their cool and waited for their moment. If even one of them had been unable to make it and had remained stranded on the beach they would probably all have come back to that one even if it meant their death.

The procedure for refloating had been clearly demonstrated and it has been put to good use many times since. Dolphins are deep-water creatures and are always vulnerable to stranding when they come into shallow water. They have difficulty registering the depth of the water in which they are swimming and can be deceived by a gradually sloping beach. On such a beach they do not become aware of their danger until the horizontal strokes of the tail fluke touch the sand. They react to this danger signal by trying to turn back into deep water. In doing so they roll over onto their sides, a position in which they are robbed of the power of forward propulsion because the lower tail fluke is obstructed by the sea floor and the upper tail fluke is flailing in the air. Unless extra depth is obtained from an incoming tide, there is no way they can by themselves regain a natural swimming stance.

In this situation it takes very little to help a dolphin or small whale into a natural swimming position and small individuals of a stranded group, not yet out of their depth, have been seen trying to help their mates. If several people can hold a dolphin steady in the tide and facing out, a moment will come when it can be launched into a wave and will find itself able to swim. The others must also be got away quickly or, at least while they are alive, it will try to come back to them.

Not all rescue attempts are successful. Mahia beach was the scene of a tragic stranding on Christmas Eve 1984. During this holiday period the usually deserted beach is thronged with holidaymakers and when six beaked whales came ashore they all joined in to try to save them. After much effort by the people on the beach and the Fisheries Officers it was realised that these whales were too big to move and a decision was made to put them down. To the horror of the holidaymakers no one knew just how to carry this out. First they tried to shoot them with large calibre rifles but were not sure exactly where to shoot. Then they tried to cut their jugular veins with machetes. The sea ran red with their blood and some of the whales appeared to be still living as they were dragged up the beach for burial by a front-end loader and tractor.

There was great public distress over this incident, a complaint to the minister and a departmental enquiry. It was discovered that these whales had been seen the afternoon before swimming about at surface level. Had this been reported to Fisheries they might have been able to avert the stranding. As it was, their procedures for whale despatch and their training methods were reviewed.

One good thing to come from the affair was the demonstration of public concern for the whales.

A stranding of 59 Sperm whales at Gisborne in 1970 could have had as horrible an outcome. Because of their great size there was no way they could be helped and I killed all of them with a lance into their jugular veins. It was more merciful than any other way and it saved the public from a distressful scene but it was an experience I would not care to repeat.

Another stranding at Te Kaha in the Bay of Plenty in 1977 had a slightly happier ending. Ninety-six pilot whales came ashore and they could all have been saved had the people on the spot known what to do.

This herd had been under surveillance for a week, swimming slowly about off Te Kaha and, finally moving closer in, they gave an indication that a member of the herd was in trouble. A lone whale grounded first and it was followed, 20 minutes later, by another nine. From then on, another group grounded about every 15 minutes until all 96 were on the beach.

Contacted by telephone, I was told that the whales were being shot as there was no way of getting them back into the sea.

"But there is a way," I insisted. "You don't need to shoot them. You can rescue them."

As we talked, the shooting was going on and by the time I had explained the technique of refloating, there were only 18 of them left. Late in the action though it was, the people on the beach were prepared to give it a go. The guns were put down, the rescue attempt was started and I was later told that the last 18 were safely got away. This stranding could have been prevented with the loss of only one whale, the key animal, the first strander. Had that whale been shot when it grounded the rest of the herd would not have stranded.

A couple of years previously, I had acted on this belief on the beach of my home town, Napier. An adult female Sperm whale stranded and was clearly to be heard transmitting distress calls in the form of a clicking noise. I tried to get the sound recorded by a radio newsman who was on the scene but the sounds of a high sea and a howling wind made it impossible. There was no hope of getting this monster off the beach and back into the sea and it could be seen that the rest of the herd were getting ready to come to her on the beach.

It was clear that she must be silenced if they were to be stopped. I made several attempts to get round to seaward to finish her off with a lance and had I not been securely roped I would have been swept out to sea to join the herd. Finally, the whale's life was ended with a rifle and her calls were silenced. The rest of the herd stopped, waited for a time, listening, then turned and swam slowly away. Had they come up onto the beach they would all have been dead whales and the city would have faced an enormous cleaning-up job. As it was it took Ministry of Works diggers and tractors to make a big enough hole in the beach and drag the carcass into it. School was out by this time and an audience of schoolchildren watched every move in the drama.

Eight years later, in June 1983, this skeleton was exhumed in a project by students of Palmerston North Teachers' Training College who wanted to present parts of it to their local museum. It took them three hours to dig it up and they found that eight years had not been long enough to get rid of the smell.

The Ahuriri Harbour on which Napier is situated is a favoured spot for dolphins and whales as well as for holidaymakers. In 1977, another solitary whale, a Goose-beaked whale, intent upon stranding, gave a large group of us a day's hard work — and a day's entertainment to the holidaymakers and children.

This whale, probably sick, was determined to come up on the beach at Westshore, Napier's favourite sandy bathing beach. I was called at the start of the action in the early morning and, with the help of local people, pushed it off every time it tried to come ashore. It cruised along the beach and the band of would-be rescuers moved along with it. Each time it tried to come in we would wade into the water, talk to it, encourage it and carefully push it off again. By the afternoon local residents and their friends were comfortably settled on their porches with cups of tea and binoculars watching me and an army of schoolchildren standing in the surf conversing with a weary whale, propping it up for a short rest against someone's legs, then persuading it to swim away again. Finally, after a long and trying day, it gave up the attempt and swam sadly off only to be found the next day, stranded and dead about three kilometres westward of this beach.

All our efforts had been in vain but we could say we had done our best to encourage it to live and the children had had a most educational day talking about and watching the whale.

A successful effort to turn a whale about and guide it to safety took place in late 1985 when a humpbacked whale got into the Sacramento river in California and swam upstream. The whale's plight got headline treatment in newspapers all over the world and I was called by a California radio station about the affair. I described to them the means by which we had turned whales about and on television I saw some of the suggestions put into practice.

I also saw useless activity such as the making of underwater noise. Baleen whales can block their eardrums with wax plugs and so do not run from noise as a toothed whale would. In a river situation the sounds would only confuse the whale further. He has a strong urge to go on and on, and every time he sounds he strikes an echo from the banks. Bridges over the river will also give a reading of an obstacle ahead. I did not see any board riders or divers in the river with the whale and had this friendly and comforting method of guidance been adopted as I suggested I think this whale might have been urged seaward faster.

Once again, the heartening feature of the affair was the

great public concern and the efforts made by public authorities to protect and help this stray whale and guide him back to his own environment.

Helicopters and army to the rescue

Because I realised the importance of making available to researchers in other countries what we were learning from the stranding incidents on the coasts of New Zealand, I passed on reports and photographs to individuals and institutions worldwide. Articles were published in all kinds of scientific and popular journals and I began to think I should have shares in the Post Office for what it cost me in postage and international telephone calls.

As interest in what we were doing grew, it became clear that within New Zealand the lessons have been well learned and more and more people are prepared to put them into action. Strandings are being averted, whales are being saved. This was well illustrated by a dolphin rescue near Nelson in 1982 when a helicopter was used in the struggle.

Denis Richardson is a farmer on a property on an inlet of Delaware Bay. He was on his way to his yards at about six o'clock in the morning when his dog started to bark and show interest in something on the beach. The farmer went down to investigate and found 21 dolphins high and dry on the beach, squeaking and grunting in their distress. Instinctively, he did the right thing; he moved among them and tried to calm them down, reassure them. He told them that they were a lot of silly buggers to get into such a situation but he would see what he could do to help. He patted them and threw water on them but then realised that time was important so, with a last reassuring word, he left them and telephoned a Ministry of Agriculture and Fisheries scientist who set the rescue process in motion.

Denis and his family collected all the sacks and covers they could find, and they telephoned the neighbours, asking them to do the same and come to the beach as fast as they could. A group of children also arrived to help and they all converged on the dolphins, carrying all manner of covers — even a bedspread.

They went to work with the buckets and sacks. They covered the dolphins against the drying power of the sun, dug holes in the beach to facilitate the collecting of water and then poured water over the covers to keep the dolphins cool. Wisely, efforts to do more than that were abandoned until more volunteers arrived, when the job of getting the dolphins into an upright position was easily achieved by organised team work. By 8 a.m. They were all righted into their natural swimming position. One rescuer with some knowledge of such things organised a bucket brigade into carrying water from the tidal shallows 50 metres away and pouring it carefully over the dolphins. Others had the vital task of staying alongside the hapless creatures and comforting them.

By 10 a.m. There were about 60 people on the beach working under the instructions of the MAF officers and staff from the Department of Scientific and Industrial Research. A Hughes 500 chopper was located not too far away. Several people were assigned to each dolphin to ready it for rescue.

The Fisheries Officers brought fine nets of the type used for the live recovery of deer by helicopter. The chopper hovered overhead, the net was laid out and one of the smaller dolphins was rolled into it. The four corners were hooked up, the signal given and the helicopter rose slowly and travelled about 800 metres to the seaward side of the sand bar. There the net was lowered into the water to a team waiting to receive it, and the dolphin was released, assisted for a time, then encouraged to swim away.

With only three minutes required for each journey, the whole herd was lifted within an hour. A few needed urging to swim away and this was done by giving their tail flukes a pump up and down. Others required rocking until their balance was restored sufficiently to resume normal, controlled swimming. The biggest of the dolphins, each weighing anything up to half a tonne, tested the power of the small helicopter, but they were lifted and deposited like the rest.

A close watch was kept on the herd and it was seen that they regrouped in the middle of the bay. A Fisheries Land-Rover patrolled the sand bar and a boat went out to keep watch and make sure the dolphins were not planning an encore.

The rescue was completed successfully primarily because one or two helpers at the scene had the natural instinct to realise the plight of marine creatures left out of the water and the initiative to implement the correct procedures to prevent the build-up of psychological stress in the dolphins' minds.

Before this extremely successful rescue I'd always refrained from advocating the use of helicopters in the rescue of marine mammals, primarily because of the noise factor and the down-draught of air from the whirling blades. The lesson learned from this incident was undoubtedly the fact that the degree of silent communication extended to these dolphins was of sufficient quality to overcome the psychological shock caused by using the chopper.

The reason for these dolphins' entry into the estuary was never established, but enquiries revealed that a large shark had been sighted in the vicinity prior to the stranding. Since dolphins tend to steer clear of sharks, it seems likely that they entered the estuary to avoid such an encounter and were trapped by the receding tide. Two juveniles were found to be much higher up the estuary beach than the rest, giving the impression that they were first to run aground, thus sealing the fate of the rest of the herd.

A similarly successful rescue in the same area was carried out in September 1985, when a family group of seven dolphins was picked up and returned to the open sea. This rescue took place in Nelson Haven, and the dolphins were lifted over the Boulder Bank into the sea. Twenty local residents, including children, spent hours standing in cold water getting them ready for the airlift.

Two teenagers were first on the scene. They found four

dolphins stranded in the mud, while three more were trapped in a pool about a metre deep. The ones in the mud were badly cut from struggling on shells and the people who came to the scene managed to get them all into the pool on the sand flat. Unfortunately, the biggest dolphin was very distressed and kept trying to beach itself again.

Three Fisheries Officers arrived next and they decided that if swift action weren't taken, this dolphin would lead all the others to re-strand on the edge of the pool. They decided to call in a helicopter. A Squirrel belonging to Helicopters New Zealand and piloted by Andy Brown arrived at about 5 p.m. The ministry officers and local people took the dolphins one by one and placed them in the net slung beneath the helicopter. Neville Buckley, Regional Fisheries Officer, waited for them on the ocean side of the Boulder Bank. All went well until the second-to-last animal was deposited. It was very upset and thrashed around a good deal until the last one, a smaller dolphin, was deposited. The two then teamed up and headed straight out to sea after the other five. It was thought they could be a mother and her calf.

What was significant in this rescue was once again the prompt action taken by the knowledgeable people who were early on the scene. The Fisheries Officers commented that these were the people who could make or break a rescue attempt, and in this case they knew what to do and did it.

Something new again in rescue work was put into practice at a stranding at Gooseberry Flats, Tryphena, on Great Barrier Island in March 1984. The Barrier has been the scene of many strandings over the years, but the obstacle which the island creates for whales was not the problem on this occasion.

On the afternoon prior to the discovery of the stranded whales by the keeper of the general store at 10.30 p.m., they were observed by other residents to be surface-swimming at speed up the harbour towards where they eventually grounded. The storekeeper woke up several residents who alerted still more people. It wasn't until daybreak that the enormity of the problem was revealed to them. One hundred and fifty pilot whales were lying on the shore.

At this time a multi-nation naval and military exercise, Operation Northern Safari, was taking place on the Barrier. Naval ships lay off the island, which hosted the headquarters of the operation. The islanders had objected to the operation taking place there and Tryphena had been the centre of the protest. Soldiers had been advised to stay away from Tryphena because of the strong objections to their presence.

When the whales came ashore, however, the servicemen offered to help. The rescue was described as an environmental sub-operation of Operation Northern Safari, its codename Operation Whale. Men from the Australian navy ship Tobruk tried to tow the whales out to sea using landing craft. They managed to get them away from the beach but couldn't prevent them from returning. Soldiers operated a bucket chain to keep the whales cool and finally brought in power pumps which greatly eased the wetting-down process. The residents, Project Jonah and Fisheries Officers struggled to keep the whales upright and facing out to sea. Some of the whales were up to six metres long and the rescuers found it hard work handling them, but they persevered throughout the day and night, in spite of seeing some die and some shot to end their misery.

At home in Taradale, hundreds of kilometres to the south, I was telephoned by my local radio station and asked to come into the studio to be interviewed about the stranding. I went on air at 10 a.m. on the second day. The station had just got the latest news from the Barrier and it was all bad. The high-powered rescue attempt was failing, primarily due to fatigue on the part of the rescuers. I was asked if I thought all the work had been a waste of time. I replied, "No! While any of them live, one just has to keep on trying no matter how exhausted and disappointed one feels."

I was then asked what I would do in the present, seemingly hopeless situation. I gave it some thought and said I would pick out the two biggest whales and get them off the beach and into the sea. I would tow them out, if necessary, for 400 metres even though they would object to leaving the others. I would take this action because it is essential to form the nucleus of a herd, somewhere for the others to swim out to when they were refloated. To tow them without hurting them I'd get a car inner-tube around the tail-stock and attach a tow-rope to that. While the tow was taking place there would need to be a couple of divers in wet-suits to keep the whales' heads above water. When it was out far enough I would attach the tow-rope to a stationary craft. Then I'd go back for the second whale, tow it out and tether it up too. I would then get the rest of the whales manhandled into the sea and pushed off towards the two big ones, hoping they would pick up their signals and swim out to them.

The interview finished and I went home. When the radio station again checked with the Barrier they found that what I'd been suggesting on the air had actually been happening at the scene of the stranding. By the time I reached home they were on the phone to tell me what was going on. The people on the spot had picked out the two biggest whales and two small ones, tethered them, then pushed the survivors into the water and herded them towards the four. By this means the last 42 animals of the herd were saved.

The radio people asked me for an explanation — was it possible, they asked, that my thoughts had been transferred to the people on the spot? I could only say that I'd seen the site of the stranding on television the night before and, as I spoke, I'd been visualising the action taking place. The radio people were convinced that somehow the images expressed on our interview had travelled further than the air-waves of a local station. It was yet another of those so-called coincidences which convince me that we are into something here that we cannot understand or explain.

The major in charge of the army rescue team apparently also thought he was into new realms. He felt the rapport which exists between animals and the people who try to help them. He reported that as the whales swam to safety one of them rolled over and lifted its flipper in the air and he got the feeling that it was saying goodbye.

The servicemen received commendations for their sterling effort and they would be the first to commend the local people who'd so strenuously resisted their coming to the island. But the investigations I carried out left no doubt that naval exercises were the cause of the whole herd's entry into the bay and subsequent stranding.

The presence of the naval ships bristling with electronic equipment standing off the outer waters of the island undoubtedly caused the herd to alter course to avoid the intense auditory pain to which the ships subjected them. That the cause was of underwater origin was demonstrated by the surface-swimming behaviour of the whales, which enabled them to hold their ear apertures above water. Caught between land and a source of electronic pulses standing off the island, the herd would have been confused and would have stranded while seeking relief by coming inshore, away from direct exposure.

The irony of this stranding was that those who were responsible for it received the honour for the part they played in the rescue of about a quarter of the original herd.

Yet another event occurred on Great Barrier Island the following year — this time it was 500 pilot whales on the beach. This stranding could probably have been averted because the herd was seen swimming around on the surface for two or three days before they came ashore. There was probably trouble in the herd; perhaps an old female or the boss bull was ill or dying. At this stage they could have been driven out to sea by small craft to landward of them herding them out gently and firmly like cattle.

A farmer's son discovered them and told his father. The farmer rang the ministry officials on the mainland and also Project Jonah. The local people of Kawa Bay, where this occurred, used the same technique as in the earlier incident — they tried to form a nucleus of the herd. At home my local radio station rang me and told me the whales were coming back as fast as they were put out. I told them the same story — get the two largest bulls and form a nucleus. Napier radio station rang Wellington and asked them to get in touch with the people on the spot, and by walkie-talkie and telephone the advice was passed on. By the time the official rescuers got to the scene the rescue was well under way. One hundred and twenty-one whales were lost but these were all dead before the rescue started.

At this time of the year pilot whales go to the warmer waters of the north for calving and mating before they go south in the summer months. Nearly every cow in this herd had a calf and the calves were very young. If some upset had caused mothers and calves to be separated it would have caused the stress which is the major cause of death in these situations.

Although most people involved feel a great sadness when stranded whales cannot be saved, every such incident can serve to add a little more to our knowledge and help us to effect a rescue next time. I believe I inherited from my father a certain skill in doctoring animals and this has proved invaluable in carrying out autopsies on dead cetacea. I have collected and cleaned many specimens taken from carcasses. My own collection is now in the Napier Natural History Museum, and I've lost track of the number of bones I have sent to overseas museums.

Sometime in 1980 I heard that the body of a Hector's beaked whale had been found near Jack and Jill Bay in the Bay of Islands, but before it could be examined by an expert of the Wellington National Museum it was washed away. The body was later found in one place while the skull and jaw were in another. This stranding received great publicity and my local newspaper published what was said to be the only known photograph of one of the world's rarest species, only two males of the species being known to science. I pointed out to them that two males of the species had stranded in Napier only three years previously, one of them on Napier's foreshore and the other, three weeks later, at the outer mole of the Port of

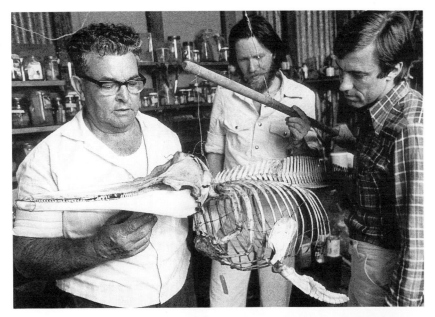

The author with two Dolphin Embassy members examining the cleaned and reassembled skeleton of a common dolphin. In the background are two specimens ready for despatch overseas.

With Richard Harrison MP, inspecting a pygmy sperm whale skull prepared by the author for display at Napier's Natural History Museum. Napier Daily Telegraph

Communication is not confined to cetacea: here Bruce Robson consorts with a young leopard seal.

Even the giant elephant seals are not dangerous, provided one can communicate with them.

A dolphin funeral procession captured on film by a Kaitaia fisherman in 1986.

The 15-metre sperm whale which was guided out through the Napier harbour entrance, accompanied by a swimmer.

The author's new interest is collecting and mounting deep-sea oddities brought in by the orange roughy fishermen. This is a large stone crab caught 30 miles off Napier at a depth of more than 1000 metres. It measures more than a metre across the legs.

The author's son, Bruce.
NZ Herald

The author and wife Sally at their 55th wedding anniversary celebration in 1984.

The Robsons with grandchildren Phillip and Abbey.

Napier. Both were dead when found.

I had identified them as Hector's beaked whales by their shape and the position of the teeth in the mandible. I photographed the head of one and the cleaned lower jaw of the other and sent the photos and a full report on both finds to the Smithsonian Scientific Event alert network in Washington. As a result, I received three reports from people who said they'd seen and identified this species, so it seems the Hector's whale is not as rare as had been thought, at least not in these waters.

A couple of years later I took the head of another whale which had died on a local beach and the action set off a furore. The local people at Te Awanga, quite rightly, reported the taking of the head. The Fisheries Officer, also rightly, set out to find and bring to punishment the culprit. It all died down when it was found that I had taken the head, that I had the right to do so as an honorary fisheries officer and that the skull was intended for the Napier Museum.

The local people on this occasion had done everything they could to save the whale. They wrapped it in blankets, and children formed a bucket chain to carry water from the sea. But the whale was found to be seriously diseased and was doomed to die anyway. I came along too late to help and I cut off the head to take away because the tide was rising and it was likely the body would be washed away.

My son Bruce found his photograph in the *New Zealand Herald* in a most compromising situation holding the enormous jaw-bone of a sperm whale. He could only protest that he was just holding it for the photographer and someone else had been at the body with a saw but had not had time to remove their illegal prize.

On this occasion, in August 1985, six sperm whales died. I was advised by Fisheries of a stranding near the Cape Palliser lighthouse, which is in the Hawke Bay Fisheries area. I was asked to go with them, but since I'd just come out of hospital after a hip replacement operation and didn't know what kind of terrain we'd be walking on, I asked Bruce to go in my place. The party left at 2 a.m. To be there by daybreak and they found the six whales dead on the beach. Parasitic worms were found in the gullet of one of them and it was deduced that this sick animal could have been the key animal which caused the stranding.

It was likely that this stranding could have been prevented because the whales had been seen swimming about offshore in a distressed state two days earlier. Unfortunately, the man who saw them didn't report it to anyone. Had he advised Fisheries when he saw them they could have taken preventive action by creating noise on the beach and using boats to chase them out to sea.

When the party from Napier arrived, someone had already been at one of the carcasses with a chainsaw and had cut out a jaw. It is no wonder they'd stayed clear when authority came, for they'd risked a fine of $15,000. There was nothing left to do but report on the situation, measure the whales, sex them and remove the rest of the lower jaws. There is little point in wasting valuable material and these would later be made available to known bone-carvers, who are now required by law to make application to the appropriate government department for their share of the spoils of strandings.

Bruce had a near-miss of an important find of fossilised whale bones in the inland ranges of the main divide which runs down the North Island. He was out pig-hunting when Maori friends told him of the remains in an inaccessible cliff-face. Not many people knew about this because the locals didn't want it to be tampered with. Shell fossils are common in the high places of the ranges, relics of the time before the young land mass of New Zealand rose up out of the sea, and this whale fossil would have been of great interest. Bruce was so keen that he engaged a helicopter to go up and photograph it, but when they arrived a landslide had taken off the face of the cliff and it now lay in the Mohaka river. They searched below at river level and came home with some pieces of rock with fossilised cetacea bone embedded in them. This was not the first such find. When the road between Napier and Taupo was being improved, whale skeleton material was found in the cuttings.

I'd only been out of hospital for a few weeks when I heard of a stranding of seven pilot whales not too far from home, just past Flat Rock at Tangoio. I was telephoned by a beach walker who'd seen the bodies on the beach. There was not much Fisheries could do. Anyway, at the time they were engaged in a private war with the fishermen on who could catch orange roughy and how much of it they could land.

Bruce drove his Land-Rover as near to the spot as he could and I walked the rest of the way, hobbling along using a walking stick and a spade. The bodies had been there for some time and were therefore not pleasant to be near. I thought the museum in Napier could use a pilot whale skull so we cleared away the sand from the head of one and severed it at the articulated joint. To get the weighty head back to the vehicle it was necessary to play Eskimos, sledging it along on a fish container. Bruce pulled and I gave him verbal encouragement.

We got it back to the Land-Rover and I'd had enough. Not so Bruce; he thought he'd go and see if he could find a better head. He found one and cut it off. He came back amongst the rocks like a figure from the Antarctic, leaning forward with the rope over his shoulder and the sledge and its cargo bumping along behind him. He was exhausted when he got his load back.

So we went home with two heads — except that we knew we dared not take them home. The most understanding wife has her breaking point, and these were very smelly heads. So we went to a farmer friend and put the heads in the pit where he disposed of his offal and dead sheep. There we went through the stinking procedure of cleaning them. We took the portable copper boiler and a large supply of firewood, as well as two packets of soap powder and some odour remover. We boiled the heads — not a nice job — for four hours. It was a long time to keep stoking the fire but, finally the two skulls and lower mandibles were in a state in which they could be stored out of sight on top of a shed for the sun to bleach and cure them.

I took the precaution of advising Fisheries that I'd taken

the skulls and that I intended them for the museum. They are now both on display, with teeth intact — one in Napier's Natural History Museum, along with all my other specimens, and the second in the Project Jonah display in Auckland.

After 25 years of observing, recording, learning and sharing it is good to note the completely changed attitude of the public to the fate of whales and dolphins. Gone is the fatalistic attitude of "How sad, poor things, why do they do it?" Now we know much more about the causes of stranding, and about the social systems and behaviour patterns of cetacea. We know that adverse weather conditions or sickness or breakdown of their social support system or danger to a member of the herd can bring them in close to shore where they are vulnerable to stranding. We can recognise the erratic swimming patterns common in a situation of confusion. An alert spotter can anticipate a stranding and get help before it begins, or even prevent it from happening at all.

In the lecture rooms and laboratories of the world's great scientific institutions, learned people go about their studies into the fascinating life of cetacea and what they are able to teach humanity in a rapidly changing world. Here in New Zealand this is no theoretical discussion. Here, it is all happening as we watch and we have learned from common-sense observation what we have to do. Our aim is to prevent strandings where possible and, if they do occur, to get safely back into the sea as many animals as possible. We make detailed reports on all such events, we collect specimens and we carry out autopsies on those which die. All this information is available to people who will never see a whale or a dolphin outside an oceanarium.

People overseas wonder why we have so many success stories in our stranding reports. One of the reasons is that we live in the middle of a natural marine laboratory; another is our caring concern for the welfare of animals and our ability to transmit this to them. I cannot stress too strongly the value of this rapport. In all the incidents I have cited the people involved have reported with a sense of wonder the warm and loving feelings which have passed between them and the animals they are trying to help. In a country in which most people have some farming connections, lessons about handling and helping are soon learned. The helicopter rescues are possible because we have highly trained pilots readily available with access to animal-lifting gear used in live-deer recovery. In every harbour there are small-boat owners ready to put their craft and themselves at the disposal of whoever is directing a rescue operation. Skindivers and board-riders will act as whale outriders with no sign of fear. The public on the beaches will work with sacks and buckets until they drop.

Those in authority are becoming confident about their ability to handle a stranding and people on the beaches are remembering a few basic rules: to watch the sea and observe any change in a herd's swimming patterns, such as milling about in circles instead of swooping forward; and to try to prevent a stranding on an open beach by making underwater noise or, in an enclosed harbour situation, by forming a physical barrier with boats.

If sperm whales come up on the beach there is, at this time and with available equipment, little to be done for them but arrange a quick death. Other sperm whales can be prevented from stranding by having the first animals on to the beach silenced.

Pilot whales — some people call them blackfish — can be rescued; so can dolphins. Keep them covered from the sun and wind and constantly wetted down. When the tide allows it, try to get them upright in the water and hold them steady in the tide, facing out. Wait for a rising wave and push them off into it. All the time let concern and consideration flow from you to reduce the stress which can kill them.

Make a report. Measure as many animals as you can. Observe their positions on the beach and draw a sketch. Report conditions of wind, sea and weather, and any pre-stranding behaviours that are observed.

By these means, we in New Zealand are showing the rest of the world that saving whales is not just a matter of putting a sticker on your car window. We are learning more all the time. When I started on this unpaid and demanding involvement 25 years ago, I had no idea I was going to be taught so much by the whales and the dolphins — and the people who care about them.

Spreading the word

While I was working at Marineland I was called upon to write a number of articles on dolphin husbandry — a subject which seems to fascinate even those who have never seen a dolphin. When our baby dolphin was born we put out a booklet titled *The Birth of a Baby Dolphin*. This passed via the hands of tourists into many countries and was reissued by a German zoological garden. From there it travelled on and was reprinted in many languages, thus drawing attention to New Zealand as good dolphin country.

After I left Marineland and my work with the dolphins, my life seemed to lose meaning. It was at this time that its course was influenced by Captain William Morzer Bruyns of the Dutch shipping line, Nedlloyd. He was captain of the first ship of that line to open trade with New Zealand. His great interest in whales and dolphins had brought him to the newly-established Marineland and he was impressed by the rapport which existed between the dolphins, the small staff and the volunteer helpers. While his ship was in port he spent most of his free time at Marineland. With three performances a day to be handled by a staff of three, we had little time to talk so after we closed at 9 p.m. The captain would come home with us for supper and some good talk.

During one conversation the subject of beach strandings came up and the captain heard with disbelief that skeleton material from such strandings was not much wanted in New Zealand museums and was lying there for the taking. He suggested that if some could be collected and prepared he would arrange with his shipping line for it to be uplifted and taken to Amsterdam University and Museum.

On his next visit I was able to tell him that I had retrieved the skull of a beaked whale which had been washed up dead on the Napier beach. I had cleaned and prepared it for him to take home to Amsterdam. As it happened, this skull turned out to be one of a rare species, not many of which were to be found in the museums of the world. It is now shown in a glass case in the mammals section of Amsterdam Museum.

From this time on our home was regularly visited by the masters of the Nedlloyd line and we had a five-day visit from Dr Pieter van Bree, curator of the Amsterdam Museum. I also formed an association with Dudok van Heel of the Haderwick Dolphinarium in the first practical attempt to establish an acceptable policy to regulate the capture and captivity of cetacea intended for public exhibition. This effort was triggered off by an inhumane practice in Europe of capturing a dolphin and carting it from town to town in a tank mounted on the back of a truck. When a dolphin died, as it very soon did under such treatment, another was captured to take its place. To my knowledge our effort was the first step towards the stringent regulations which are in force today to protect captive dolphins in dolphinariums throughout the world and was the forerunner of the Marine Mammals Protection Act now common in many countries.

In 1972 Dudok van Heel, who was fearful of the possible extinction of dusky dolphins, had asked for the capture and delivery to Haderwick Dolphinarium of six specimens of the species to allow him to set up a programme of breeding in captivity. Arrangements to accede to his request were well under way, with air transport plans made, when the project was called off. Deep-frozen dolphin carcasses previously sent by me to Holland had been sent to the Atomic Research Centre at Utrecht to check on the mercury and persistent pesticide level in the liver and brains of dolphins which had died in the nets of fishing boats in Hawke Bay. I received the result of the analysis and was shocked at the high level found of these toxic substances.

This revelation of the deteriorating state of our waters

led to a great deal of effort in trying to convince the Ministry of Agriculture and Fisheries of the seriousness of the situation and finally the use of the persistent pesticide DDT was stopped in New Zealand. There was no doubt but that the lethal combination of these pesticides and methol mercury in our waters was taking its toll on the whales and dolphins and affecting their ability to keep clear of the fishing nets. Toxic waste was pouring into the sea by way of run-off into rivers and waterways from chemically treated paddocks. It was ingested by the small fishes which, in turn, were eaten by the larger ones . . . and so returned to us.

Many articles about the New Zealand situation were written in overseas publications. I supplied material for many of them and so gained a reputation as an expert in the field. In 1976 my book *Thinking Dolphins, Talking Whales* was published, and this brought about another surge of interest in what was happening in New Zealand and in my theories about the matter. My success with non-verbal communication was of particular interest and a string of people engaged in studies into the subject came to Taradale to stay with us. They were frequently sponsored on these trips by educational or conservation bodies.

Jim Nollman, from the Animal Welfare Institute of Washington, stayed with us for three weeks. He brought his tape recorder and his recorded interviews led to publication in the *New Age* magazine, an American monthly with a readership of half a million. On the front page was a picture of me conversing with a dolphin. Horace Dobbs, author of *Follow a Wild Dolphin*, came from England. Steve Dawson, a New Zealander and an expert in the study of Hector's dolphins, has been a regular visitor and has recently published the *New Zealand Whale and Dolphin Digest*.

Professor Patricia Hindley came from Simon Fraser University in Vancouver; her subject is communications research. During her stay with us she was impressed by the quantity of material and notes I had accumulated and on her return to Canada she contacted Bill Rossiter in

America and Nick Carter in South Africa, both of whom share an interest in the subject of communications. Between them they instigated a proposal to raise funds for the three of them to make a 10-week visit to our home to correlate and record for distribution all my research material. Unfortunately they were not able to finance the venture.

Bob Loader and Tristram Miall, with their film crew, stayed with us during the filming of their documentary *Stranded*. After my appearance in this film (featured in the *Our World* series) and my involvement in the Hardy Jones documentary film *Island on the Edge*, interest grew to unmanageable proportions. In 1984 my second book, *Strandings*, was published overseas and brought a further increase in correspondence. Nick Carter, an Englishman living in South Africa and a dedicated conservationist, offered to edit it and Professor Graham Saayman, Head of the Department of Psychology at the University of Cape Town, wrote a foreword and offered it to his own publishers, Science Press. As a textbook on the stranding problem it has been well received in other countries and favourably reviewed in important scientific publications. Unfortunately it has not yet found a distributor in New Zealand.

Other visitors have included people from the American Dolphin Embassy scheme, Telecommunications Systems Los Angeles, Interspecies Communications, Project Jonah USA and the Sydney TV School. Dr John Allen, who managed Marineland in Napier for a time, was a frequent visitor and had a deep interest in alternative methods of communication.

I have been involved in the making of many of the films about dolphins and whales now being shown around the world. Sometimes I took part in the film; on other occasions I was retained as adviser. Among the many friendships developed was with the North Wind Undersea Institute of City Island, New York. This group made a film called *Whale Rescue* which was dedicated to me and shown at the Whales Alive Conference where it won an award. The Whale Rescue Team of the North Wind Institute have

114

developed rescue gear capable of handling the big whales without injury and a team of eight, led by Captain Michael Sandlofer, went out on an equipment-testing expedition. With the permission and co-operation of the Mexican Government, they made a land, sea and air search of the coastline on which young Scamperdown whales have regularly beached. Until the development of this rescue gear there was little any rescuer could do to return these half-tonne calves to their ocean environment.

The team found no live whales but it did find five dead calves and an unusual number of dead older whales. The equipment was tested out on a large whale found on its back in swampy terrain and it was found possible to ready the 10-metre, 17-tonne whale for release without apparent injury. The North Wind team had the satisfaction of knowing that with their equipment whales which had previously been doomed to die on the beach could now be saved, even without the use of any motorised equipment or chains.

I was kept informed of this development and generously given a share of the credit for the achievement. It was gratifying to know that the knowledge we have gained in New Zealand was being successfully applied elsewhere.

Another film in which I played an advisory role was made by Dr Simon Cotton of Auckland on the orca or killer whale. Dr Cotton, who owns a large boat, loves the sea and its creatures, especially the orca, the largest of the dolphins, the fiercest and perhaps the most intelligent. They are visually dramatic in their stark black and white markings and are carnivorous. Dr Cotton, himself an underwater photographer, teamed up with others of similar interest when they decided to get in amongst the orcas to make an underwater film. They had found the orcas friendly enough creatures when they came alongside the boat but they had heard about those big jaws full of sharp teeth tearing seals to pieces and swallowing them.

I assured them that the orcas would only be dangerous when in a feeding frenzy and that it was important for them not to upset the boss in any way as if he was upset he would take action to protect his herd. If assured approaches were made in a friendly fashion, the orcas would reciprocate. My only advice was — do it slowly, take your time, don't make an abrupt approach.

The film was made in the Bay of Islands. Once the film crew overcame their fear and generated friendship they found they had no trouble swimming in amongst the orcas.

In 1980 I was invited to a four-day seminar held by the International Whaling Commission at the Smithsonian Institute in Washington D.C. The subject under discussion was the behaviour and migration patterns of cetacea and it seemed as though I was one of the few there with practical experience of the subject. Everyone else, heavy with degrees, appeared to be working out of university and research laboratories. When I found that I had been allocated only 20 minutes to speak and show slides, I thought it was strange to have brought me so far and at such expense for such a short contribution. Had I stayed at home where the matters under discussion were actually happening, I could, with the money allocated for my travel, have hired a helicopter and a cameraman and gone out to look for some new material for them. However, the few of my books which were available for sale were snapped up so it had its bright side.

The book got a good plug from an unexpected direction. I arrived in Washington after a continuous, and sleepless, journey of 36 hours, and went to the hotel shown on my bookings, only to be told that I was not, in fact, booked in. Would I please stand by while they tried to make alternative arrangements? I would and did. I dropped into the nearest available seat to wait and found myself sitting on a thick magazine. I rescued the magazine and began to look at it.

It took my dulled brain a moment to realise that I was looking at a picture of me kneeling at the edge of a pool deep in communication with a cheerful-looking dolphin. The long accompanying article was the one — already referred to — resulting from Jim Nollman's three-week stay at our home. I had not known the article was written,

116

let alone accepted. I read it through and was not altogether happy with it. A great deal was left unsaid on the subject of inter-species communication and I felt Jim had not asked the questions which would have elicited the right answers. However, I was interested to see him refer to my book *Thinking Dolphins, Talking Whales* as "an underground best-seller", although puzzled as to why "underground". It went well over the counter in New Zealand.

When my turn came to speak at the seminar, the audience found it a change to speak to someone with first-hand experience of cetacea in the wild and, although the red stop light was put on me several times, I kept on answering their questions and made a mess of their timetable. The upshot of it was that I was offered a $75,000 contract for a six-month lecture tour. This I declined because too much material and learning experience would be going to waste while I was away from home. As I've said before, I live in the best marine laboratory in the world. So I packed up and went happily back to my unpaid work.

I missed out on two further important international meetings to which I was invited as principal speaker in 1981 — the first, organised by the R.S.P.C.A., in Brighton, England, on the subject of whale strandings, was cancelled through lack of funds; the second, sponsored by the Connecticut Cetacea Society, I had to forego on the grounds of ill-health. Ill-health, however, did not prevent me from making lengthy submissions to the Select Committee considering the composition of the Marine Mammals Protection Act.

Lack of finance had become a great problem, and threatened to bring my involvement in the work to a finish, for we had finally come to an end of our life savings. The cause of the whales had swallowed it all though, because I had maintained a worldwide correspondence, the Post Office had taken its share. However, several overseas institutions, including the Animal Welfare Institute of Washington, the Connecticut Cetacea Society, the Melbourne Museum, sent some help

117

to meet expenses, and somehow the work went on.

The most generous gift of all came when things were at a very low ebb for me. I had gone into hospital for a hip replacement and ended up having a stomach by-pass operation. While I was at my lowest, I received a grant from Project Jonah of $5000. Then the Ministry of Agriculture and Fisheries issued me with a Marine Mammals Protection Officer's ticket, which gave me authority to intervene when I saw fit in the conduct of a stranding rescue action. These two signs of recognition gave me the will and determination to live, to get better and to get back to work.

Mental communication — how does it work?

Animals communicate with one another without words. Can we learn to do the same?

Some of us can and I believe I am one such person. I call this faculty Telepathic Image Portrayal (T.I.P.). Scientists are very wary of it because it has not been proved in research projects or explained in learned theses. It is not easy to find the words to explain that words can be done without. I've been interviewed many times on the subject and have never been satisfied with the result of the interview. The interviewer poses questions and one tries to answer them but the exchange of words rarely gets to the heart of the matter. The more we search for the right words, the further we get from an explanation.

Since the publication of my first book I have had many requests for more information from people all around the world. I have always tried to respond but it is no easy task being in the position of both researcher and researched, perhaps comparable to that of the lawyer who takes his own case.

It is easier for me to give examples. The most dramatic incident, and the one involving the most people, was the time when I was out in the boat on one of the few occasions when I was without radio. The engine broke down miles from port and in a howling gale. The third anchor failed to prevent drift and I began to think I was on my way to Peru in fast time before a driving wind. There was little I could do to help myself except to concentrate on sending repeated thought messages to my wife, Sally. I concentrated particularly hard at midday for I knew exactly where she would be at that time; she would be at home getting lunch for the boys.

Although I was not expected home for several hours, Sally got the message and she telephoned the fish shed to tell them that she thought I was in trouble. Not knowing my position they alerted the airways to look out for me, and also radioed other fishing boats to keep an eye open for me.

Two of my fishermen friends picked up the message on their radios, returned to port immediately, discharged their catches and put back to sea again. I had no way of notifying my position as the flares I was carrying could not be seen in the daytime but I knew that these two boats would be involved in the search, so I concentrated my thoughts on the two skippers, one of whom was an old schoolfriend.

The surface of the sea was a boiling mass of white-caps and the chance of my eight-metre craft being seen from a distance was remote indeed. I knew that when they came I would be able to see them long before they could see me. After six hours the gale abated a little and the three anchors stopped the drift. I stared into the direction my compass told me was home. At first I wasn't sure; I had to look intently to convince myself that, yes, I could see the shape of a wheelhouse above the waves, then the mast and eventually the hull of a vessel which could not yet see me lying so low in the water.

I continued sending out mental impulses and the boat, without altering course, came straight towards me. I recognised it as the boat of my old schoolmate coming with the wind astern of him. It was a great relief when he signalled with a puff of black exhaust smoke that he'd sighted me. He soon closed the gap between us and came up to accept the tow-rope I had ready.

Luckily the long haul back to port was directly into the wind which allowed me to take advantage of the shelter provided by the larger craft as she ploughed into the white-caps. Within half an hour of starting the tow, the gale dropped away and the sea calmed. Darkness was falling as we reached port.

Although I knew my wife would have picked up the thought message that I was safe, my skipper friend used the conventional method of communication. He radioed port and the fish shed people telephoned Sally to tell her I was safely in tow.

After we'd tied up at the wharf I asked the skipper how he'd known where to look for me in that boiling sea. His reply was short and precise: "We were hooked into some sort of beam."

Then he added his conclusion. "Strange things happen at sea."

Long before I came to know dolphins I knew I had the ability to transmit mental images but I never questioned it. We all know a few people who have some form of E.S.P. but they rarely puzzle over the how and why of it. We accept that medical science does not know of what the mind is capable; they only know that we do not use it to its full capacity. It was only when I came into regular contact with wild dolphins at sea that I began to search for an answer. Out in the boat I could mentally leave my world and its problems behind as I had physically left them behind. I could experience calmness and tranquility and give the dolphins my undivided attention, often neglecting my work to do so.

Dolphins, more than any other mammal, show superiority in thought transfer. Never in my long association with terrestrial animals have I seen such speed of response and such pleasure in responding. I came to believe that animals such as dogs and horses have been in human company for so long that the are conditioned to our ways, and people are convinced that the only way these non-speaking animals can comprehend is by listening to our spoken commands.

It was quite clear that the dolphins were able to read my thoughts and were well on the way to responding to them before I had time to utter a word. I knew that dolphins had the ability to echo-locate by sending out an impulse from that big, brainy forehead of theirs and receiving back an echo which somehow gave them an accurate picture of something outside their vision. I could easily accept that this had developed over the ages to compensate for their limited visual range in the sea. Now it seemed to me that they were capable of sending out an impulse and getting back an echo-image from my mind. I don't know what takes place inside their heads but I think of their minds as something like a video screen onto which images are formed.

I would sit day after day alone in my boat, alone with the dolphins. It was the best possible research laboratory, better than anything all the government grants in the world could set up. I asked myself a thousand times what was this process of communication, what powered it and how could humans achieve it?

I was horrified when I thought about attempts being made in America and in Russia to teach dolphins to speak words — to introduce them to our slow and cumbersome method of conveying thoughts, so open to misunderstanding — when their own method is so swift and accurate, and so much more efficient. I studied my own thought processes as closely as I studied the dolphins'. I realised that until then I, too, had taken it for granted that the animals were responding to my words and now here were the dolphins, squeaking and jabbering away for fun but relying on something much faster for communication.

I have never ceased to be astonished by the speed at which an image is transferred from one mind to another. No one but the person originating the thought can have any idea of the swiftness of the response. Scientists tell us of impulses circling the globe in one-seventh of a second. I feel we are dealing with such instantaneous responses not only in the dolphins but also in some living human beings. I call it the miracle image.

I've tried to analyse what goes on in my mind at the instant of delivery of a non-verbal message. I compare the form of thought of persons who use language as their medium with the forms I use when trying to communicate with animals unable to use the word-form. At the start, the two approaches are similar in my mind. In human-to-human communication a thought or request is presented in words and the words are selected according to the estimated vocabulary of the recipient. If it is a child I will use short words with which I know the child is familiar. In human-animal communication the thought will be changed into non-verbal images which relate to what I know the animal knows — its habitat and lifestyle. It helps to think of the human mind as a film projector loaded with developed, silent film. The picture it gives will appear on a screen in the mind of the dolphin. This is the first phase.

The second phase concerns the receptivity of the dolphin's mind. It must be open to receive the image and it will not be so unless the animal is happy and at peace.

The third phase is to ensure that the sender of the image does so in genuine concern and respect. A normal friendly approach to Horace in our early involvement was a light tap on the side of the boat. Horace would usually come to the side of the boat to investigate the sound, head out of the water, mind interested and receptive. If an image were then thrown at him — hitting him with it was my term — he would usually oblige by doing what was being requested of him.

I use the word "requested" because there is absolutely no way a wild dolphin can be forced to comply with the wishes of a human. If it suits him he'll comply. If he doesn't feel like it he won't. The dolphins at Monkey Mia enjoying the pleasures of hand-feeding were proof of that. But when phase one, a clear, swift transmission, and phase two, clear receptivity, come together on the same wavelength, the dolphin will usually respond.

Since humans are tied into the use of words it is likely that words will not be left out and an integrated image/spoken word will result. This can have an interesting side effect. At the start everything hinges on the image, and to send it out it is important that it is not tangled up in word interpretation as it goes. Fortunately, the direct image is so fast that it is being delivered as it forms and before the words can form. If the words come afterwards, as they frequently do, they may deliver a different image to be tested against the first.

It is very difficult to lie successfully to a person who is on the mental image wavelength. The words spoken may not match up with the mental image received and the recipient will know that the first image is the reliable message. So I knew that to form mental images I must exercise sufficient mental control to ignore any form of words and I knew that calmness of mind was necessary for this.

There is built into human nature a basic longing for something more, to be part of something greater than self. In the search for this something, from traditional Christian prayer through yoga and its like to transcendental meditation, the first instruction of a spiritual director or guru is to clear the mind of its clutter of words and thoughts, of its ceaseless churning, to abandon all negative and unloving thoughts and, in clearness and quiet, await enlightenment.

When I asked myself what kind of creatures were the dolphins to so completely achieve the right frame of mind, I found they match up well to the advice given to seeking humans. They are happy, trusting, loving, secure in a good social system, at one with their environment; they never attack one another — indeed, they are prepared to die for one another. I have referred to dolphins saving whales and humans in the sea. I will deal shortly with some accounts of grieving mother dolphins carrying their dead babies on their backs. I recall many examples of the affectionate feelings which automatically rise between dolphins and people. I know they are a spirit of good in the world.

I often ask myself why we human beings have to learn everything the hard way. We have to be bitten by a dog or scratched by a cat, kicked by a horse or humiliated by words before we can grasp a message which is staring us in the face. The problem lies in our inability to achieve compatibility of thought with one another, an inability to keep open the channels, the wavelengths on which thoughts can pass.

Husbands and wives often communicate non-verbally. They can travel distances in a car without speaking but contentedly sharing sights and thoughts; they can pass unspoken messages to one another in a crowd. They are compatible, motivated by love and concern for one another; the channels for transference of thought are open.

I am convinced that our relationship with Horace was successful because it was based on a genuine concern for his welfare and respect for his right to be himself and respond in a way natural to him. These sentiments are present in all animal lovers and are much more important than scientific training, which is often actually a hindrance. People who live close to nature and close to animals are open to fresh leads into new knowledge and less afraid of criticism.

I make this attempt at an explanation to help those people who have written to me asking about mental communication. To sum up the method of communicating with dolphins:

• The person transmitting the request must be motivated by genuine concern and care.

• The dolphin must be in a receptive frame of mind. If it has food or sex on its mind it will be oblivious to all else, and you will have to wait.

• If you speak to the dolphin at all, regard words as just tones, not meanings. Some tones of voice he will find pleasurable and reassuring but if he doesn't like your tone you will lose his attention. He has no time to waste on what does not give him pleasure.

• Use gestures that are friendly and not abrupt or frightening.

• When you form a mental image which you want to convey to him, remember that you're dealing with an animal in his natural environment, not trying to have a philosophical discussion with him. You are trying to get him to do something you want him to do so limit your mental image to things within his experience and knowledge. When you form a picture of the boat, it must be the boat as he sees it, a hull and propeller in the water and friendly faces looking down from it. If, when you picture the boat you visualise it as you see it — the cabin and the engine room — you are wasting your time. You are in areas beyond his knowledge. When I wanted Horace to go out of the inner harbour into the bay, I made a mental picture of him swimming flat out along the channel towards the heads. Within seconds he'd be doing just that.

The great unanswered question is — what triggers off the picture transfer? What takes that image from my mind directly to that of the dolphin so that it immediately performs the action I have pictured? I'm sure that activating this impulse is like throwing a switch to bring into operation a true physical force, as real as radio waves or electricity. I don't know what activates it but determination, compassion and concern seem to be involved. Human beings constantly report feeling a charge of something akin to love emanating from the whales and dolphins with which they have had contact.

In its normal life in the sea, a dolphin navigates by way of its sonar, an intricate system which forms its mental pictures. It sends out impulses, waves echo back to its brain and it has a picture. I ask myself — when an image passes from a human to a dolphin, how much is it the result of that human's effort, and how much is the dolphin picking up the image in the same way as it reads the layout of the sea and coastline around it?

What is the dolphin ability? Can we protect the dolphins and whales from our own destructiveness long enough for us to learn it from them? In the dolphinarium in Japan the language barrier between me and the Japanese was formidable but I had some success in communicating with the dolphins. If we could cultivate mental communication, perhaps we could find an escape from the killing traps of misunderstanding caused by our use of words. When I speak, my words go through the screen of the listeners' minds, through the filter of their hopes and fears, inhibitions and frustrations. What they think they hear is quite often different from what I think I said and every person has picked up a different emphasis. Words have pushed us away from one another.

Is there a better way? I believe there is and that the dolphins and whales can teach us. When we work to save them we are, in a sense, acting to save ourselves.

In concluding this chapter, I'd like to impress upon readers that I do not suggest this form of thought transfer could replace the orthodox, verbally expressed form. However, now that I have identified the element responsible for the successful integration of the two forms, I feel it would be both selfish and unjust to withhold the clues associated with its successful implementation.

The irony of the situation is that it has taken me until now to explain in words that which I have used successfully all my life, primarily, because until now, I've not had the time, nor could I find the necessary tranquility to dig deeper into the depth of the mind in search of the clues from which logical conclusions can be assimilated.

The utopia of mother love

On three separate occasions in recent years I've been the grateful recipient of eyewitness accounts of a most touching and sad dolphin behaviour. All three events relate to the reactions of bereaved mothers of newly born calves, and the family groups to which the victims belonged.

The first reported incident occurred off the Australian coast when a very young calf became entangled in a gill net and died before it could be released. On being rolled out of the net the calf was picked up by the mother who balanced the limp corpse on her body between her blowhole and dorsal fin. For several hours she carried her dead baby in this fashion, swimming just below water level, until she reached shallow water. She released her precious cargo there, and swam out of the shallows to rejoin her waiting family group, which then left the scene.

The second incident also occurred in Australian waters, and was reported by a commercial fisherman who was sailing his yacht in a large, deep estuary. There he observed the unheard-of behaviour of a group of continuously surface-swimming dolphins. The group of nine was led by a mother who carried a newly born corpse balanced in front of her dorsal fin. The little body pushed up a bow-wave as the mother moved in a straight line towards a gradually sloping sandy beach some miles ahead.

The fisherman noted, to his surprise, that his presence caused no apparent concern, so was encouraged to join what was obviously a funeral procession. After one and a half hours the cortege came to within 400 metres of the beach and stopped. After a minute or two of obvious communication amongst all members of the group, the mother proceeded alone towards the beach, carrying her dead infant. When she was in only about a metre of water she allowed the corpse to float free. After gently nuzzling the baby's head with her beak several times she slowly turned seawards and rejoined the family group, whereupon another brief consultation was held amongst the herd members. The entire group then turned and headed back the way they'd come, this time swimming normally.

The most recently witnessed event took place in 1986 on the upper north-eastern coast of New Zealand. While towing a trawl net in shark-infested waters over five miles off shore, a commercial fisherman observed a group of dolphins following a bow-wave made by a semi-submerged object. Puzzled, he locked the helm and went up on deck for a clearer view. He saw the head and front end of a dolphin surface to blow before disappearing again just behind the mysterious bow-wave, which he then realised with amazement was the prone body of a newborn dolphin calf.

Grabbing his camera from the wheelhouse he went forward and managed to take a remarkable shot as the mother surfaced to blow, revealing her sad little burden. Unable to follow because of the trawl, he watched the group head on a straight course landwards until they were out of sight. I was the fortunate recipient of the one-in-a-million print of the grieving mother carrying her infant to its burial place.

Now that this behaviour has been sufficiently authenticated, the question is, "Where was the mother taking the dead calf?" To those who have studied these creatures it is obvious that the mother was well aware of the area for which she'd set a straight course; in each case it was shorewards of the area where the death occurred.

The second question is, "Why was she going to so much trouble to get the corpse to the pre-ordained spot?" The logical answer is that the inshore waters are far less prone to shark infestation than the deep. Had the corpses been left in the deep waters they'd have undoubtedly been torn to pieces and eaten.

Nothing is impossible . . .

Now, at the age of 74, I have achieved that which I thought impossible 25 years ago. And I find myself racing against time to complete and bring up to date what will be my last book. It has long been my desire to impart what I have learned from my dedicated study of and research into natural phenomena, the facts of which are as yet little known, even to science.

I would also like to share with others the personal satisfaction associated with the successful publication and worldwide distribution of my two previous books, *Thinking Dolphins, Talking Whales* in 1976, and *Strandings* in 1984.

This book is my autobiography, but it also includes the personally rewarding events which have proved beyond doubt that many of the accepted theories relating to whales and dolphins are wrong, especially the reasons hitherto accepted for strandings on sandy beaches.

Evidence that whales are *not* committing suicide is contained in this last chapter, which demonstrates that not only can the whales be rescued; better still, they can be prevented from grounding, provided those living near likely stranding sites are sufficiently enlightened to advise the appropriate people (marine mammals are now the Department of Conservation's responsibility) of the presence of whales inshore.

The following two little-publicised events took place within six and a half kilometres of my home base, in Horace territory. To my way of thinking, these two incidents are as important as was the first successful rescue of 80 pilot whales in early 1965. That particular stranding and its ultimate outcome set the pattern for the

130

numerous successes which have been accomplished since. The Great Barrier Island rescue of 400 out of 500 pilot whales in 1985 was the most successful to date in terms of numbers saved. Many successful rescues have been accomplished on herds of up to 80, sometimes with the loss of only three or four whales.

The first of the two *prevented* strandings occurred in 1983 at the Bight, a natural whale trap at the southern end of Westshore Beach. The whale concerned was a fully grown, 15-metre-long bull Sperm. The massive creature was first seen by beach residents, swimming south about 800 metres off-shore. As he approached the southern end of the beach he was confronted by an outcrop of rock which is covered by water at high tide. As intending rescuers were preparing to get to the scene the whale tried to get over the shallow reef but got stuck. He managed to free himself by turning shorewards where there was considerably less rock formation.

By this time, wetsuit-clad rescuers were arriving. Two people were positioned, one on either side of the Sperm's head at eye level, and a third was stationed aft of the tail flukes. At first the whale refused to budge, but when the diver at the tail was asked to give the flukes a gentle kick, the huge creature began to move forward.

At this point, two surf-ski paddlers arrived on the scene, and they were asked to take position by the eyes, two and a half metres from the huge snout. By doing this, the surf-ski riders were able to guide the whale. If he veered off course to the left, the rider on that side hit the surface of the water with his paddle, and this was enough to make the creature straighten up.

By this method the monster was guided back the way he'd come until he was clear of the reef. When this was accomplished he was coaxed to change direction out to sea, and he eventually cleared the end of the breakwater mole. He then set a course for a point off Cape Kidnappers before diving. After he'd been observed to surface and blow four times without altering course, he was left to go his own way.

This triumphant effort was surpassed three years later,

on 14 January 1987, though by this time my lack of mobility prevented my playing an active part in the rescue work.

On the clear sunny morning in question I received a phone call at 8 a.m. To alert me to the presence of some 25 Sperm whales close inshore in the same potential stranding area at the southern end of Westshore Beach. The caller was Rosamond Rowe, my understudy of several years, during which time she had received considerable practical and theoretical tuition in whale and dolphin rescue. The concern in her voice conveyed to me the urgency of the situation, and I knew why as soon as she told me where the whales were. She said she'd alert the Fisheries Department and my son Bruce if she could locate him.

"I'll go straight to Westshore," I told her, and she was gone. I passed the word to Sally as I grabbed my walking stick, and called to her to bring the binoculars while I opened the garage doors. As Sally handed me the glasses I said, "They're Sperms," and, to my surprise, she hopped into the car with me. The traffic lights were with us and within 10 minutes we were at the beach.

There, before our eyes, was an indescribable once-in-a-lifetime spectacle. The grandeur of the scene was obviated somewhat by the seriousness of the danger they'd put themselves in by coming so close to the gently sloping, sandy beach. The gracefulness of their gleaming bodies surging through the surface of the calm sea will live in my memory forever. Sal was speechless; this was her first sight of a herd of whales.

I summed up the situation in a flash. They were indeed Sperms — a harem herd consisting of adult females and their progeny of all ages. There was no adult bull, which was no surprise to me at that time of year. My interest then switched to concern that they were only 400 metres from shore and getting closer. Their bellies must have been almost rubbing on the sandy bottom.

I found what I was looking for when I scanned the water with binoculars (a donation from Amsterdam Museum for this very purpose, in recognition of my contributions of whale material to them). On the first sweep with those powerful glasses I spied the undoubted culprit, or "key" whale, a name I've given to those in a herd which upset its normal lifestyle. Unsurprisingly, it was a juvenile of about seven metres who would still be dependent on its mother for sustenance. Unlike its herd-mates it was lying still, apart from occasionally surfacing to blow before partly submerging again. It was obviously ailing as it was about 800 metres due east of the herd and precariously close to the outer edge of the shallow reef.

As I handed Sal the glasses to have a look at the calf, all the horror of my first experience of mass stranding, a harem herd of 59 Sperms, welled up in my mind. I didn't want a repeat of that ghastly episode, when I'd been forced to lance every one. Sal must have picked up my thoughts. She laid down the glasses and said, "For God's sake, Fisheries, hurry up."

Instinctively I stared beyond the ailing calf to the end of the wharf where the patrol boat was berthed and, to my relief, saw that very boat come into view. The binoculars confirmed that the two figures up front were Ros and her husband, Allan.

"Give her the gun," I urged, with one eye on the herd and the other on the boat, which instantly increased speed and set a course for the Bight. Those aboard the patrol boat knew the locality well and they made good time.

I knew that Ros was well versed in the importance of first identifying and dealing with the key whale, but I was a little apprehensive that she might be distracted by the spectacle of the herd, massed together, blowing plumes of vapour into the air, and not realise that the calf was a way apart.

Ros, too, must have developed six eyes that day in order to sum up the situation. Immediately the bow of the boat passed the point which had previously obscured her view of the key whale, I "hit" Ros with the mental image of the calf's position in respect to hers on the boat. As if by magic her arm pointed straight at the calf, and as quickly the boat changed course. It slowed almost to a stop and drifted up to the sick whale.

Get between it and the edge of the reef, I mentally urged. Again, as if by magic, the patrol boat manoeuvred into the desired position. Slowly but forcefully, it pressured the calf into moving the 800 metres or so to the milling herd, which only required one of its members to get into shallow water and lie on its side to trigger off a major stranding.

Good on you, Ros, was my unspoken thought. You've learned well. The calf, still swimming on the surface, joined up with the herd.

"What now?" asked Sal as I sighed with relief.

"They'll have to set up a series of patrols between the herd and the beach, and move in closer to the milling herd until it decides to move seawards. Then the boat should act as a drover does when moving cattle. If necessary the direction of the herd can be changed by appropriate manoeuvring on the part of the patrol. At all times great care should be exercised to avoid rushing the herd, especially in this case because the sick calf may need a spell more often that is normal."

This very scenario unfolded before our eyes. We stayed and watched the patrol boat and its precious charges as they moved far out to sea where the ailing youngster would be able to die without signing the death warrant of the entire herd by stranding while alive.

Although I had no radio communication with Ros or the boat, her judgement of what was necessary in every phase of a tricky operation was much more than one could expect. Not only was I proud of the way she handled the entire situation, including the speed with which she got a response from Fisheries, but I felt a great responsibility had been lifted from my shoulders. I realised that, in partnership, she and Bruce were worthy of carrying on the work I'd begun more than two decades previously. I can now rest assured that stranding whales in this area will continue to be accorded the best treatment possible.

This episode, I believe, sheds light on the tremendous advantages of being able to fall back on Telepathic Image Portrayal as a means of successful communication when the accepted, orthodox forms are not available. In this case the stage was set for the use of T.I.P., so great was the concern for the welfare of these creatures by both the transmitter and recipient. It is this that makes Telepathic Image Portrayal possible.

Until my time to depart this earth, I'm sure I'll remain the most inquisitive student of the logic of nature's ways. On occasions I have adopted a very impatient attitude towards some scientists who persistently refuse to accept facts established from years of repeated practical experience. I attribute my acquired knowledge to my inherited quest for enlightenment and a determination to succeed whatever the barriers.

My involvement in gaining and imparting knowledge of things natural has been so personally rewarding that I'd happily do it all over again. None of it would have been possible without the support of my supremely tolerant wife, Sal, or the help of our children and scores of friends.

Having accepted that my physical mobility is now limited to coping with the outside chores around the house, I have taken the opportunity to use my spare time to preserve and mount for museum exhibition specimens of fish, coral and crabs from deep-water trawling operations 45 nautical miles off our coast.

Our son Bruce, who is a "cargo-ologist" (wharfie) at the Port of Napier, and friendly with orange roughy fishermen, alerted me to the availability of rare deep-water specimens, which he now brings to me for preserving and mounting. I have developed a preserving technique whereby I am able to retain the natural colour and lustre of the crabs, fish and coral, the whole operation taking place in my backyard shed.

In this way I am able to continue to bring the wonders of the deep to landlubbers. Because it is a labour of love, the fishermen are extremely cooperative in supplying me with these specimens, which I pass on to schools to enhance the knowledge of young people.

If I manage to instil in the young a thirst for the wonders of nature, I will feel I have travelled my path to some purpose.